MUSSOLINI
THE LAST 10 DAYS
A NEW INVESTIGATION

MALCOLM TUDOR

Uncovering the race between SOE, OSS,
and the partisans to kill or capture
Italy's Fascist dictator

EMILIA PUBLISHING

First edition published in 2022 by Emilia Publishing

Newtown, Powys, SY16 2DR

www.emiliapublishing.com

emiliapublishing@btinternet.com

Copyright © Malcolm Tudor 2022

British Library Cataloguing in Publication Data: A catalogue record for this book is available from the British Library.

ISBN 978-1-915292-86-5

The right of Malcolm Tudor to be identified as the author of this work has been asserted by him in accordance with the Copyright, Designs and Patents Act 1988.

All rights reserved. No part of this publication may be reproduced, stored in a retrieval system or transmitted in any form or by any means, electronic, mechanical, photocopying, recording or otherwise, without prior permission in writing from the publisher

- Printed in the UK by Biddles Books -

CONTENTS

Glossary 5

About the Author 7

Acknowledgements 7

Author's Note 8

1. Mussolini's Nightmare 11
2. Facing his Enemies 16
3. Fascists in Flight 22
4. The Lake Partisans 32
5. The Famous Roadblock 40
6. The Enemy Convoy 45
7. The Capture of Mussolini 54
8. The German Surrender 61
9. Moving Mussolini 68
10. Turning Back 78
11. The Couple's Last Night 83
12. Partisan Plots in Milan 86
13. Colonel Valerio 92
14. The Couple's Last Day 104
15. The Execution 106

16. More Killings 112

17. The American Investigation 118

18. The Eyewitnesses 123

19. Suspicious Deaths 129

20. OSS Agents (1) 135

21. OSS Agents (2) 141

22. OSS Agents (3) 145

23. SOE Agents (1) 154

24. SOE Agents (2) 161

25. SOE Agents (3) 164

26. Allied Orders 174

27. General Cadorna's Orders 177

28. Partisan Orders 180

29. Who Ordered the Killings? 186

30. The Italian Solution 193

Appendix A: The Churchill-Mussolini Correspondence 201

Appendix B: Churchill's Writings on Mussolini 203

Appendix C: Personnel File of Leo Valiani 204

Endnotes 209

Leading Personalities 215

Bibliography 222

GLOSSARY

AFHQ Allied Force Headquarters, Mediterranean Theatre

CIA Central Intelligence Agency, United States

CLN *Comitato di liberazione nazionale:* National Liberation Committee

CLNAI *Comitato di liberazione nazionale Alta Italia:* National Liberation Committee for Upper Italy

CVL *Corpo volontari della libertà:* Corps of Volunteers of Liberty, fighting forces of the Resistance

FO Foreign Office, United Kingdom

GL *Giustizia e Libertà:* Justice and Liberty organisation whose members founded the Action Party in 1942

GNR *Guardia nazionale repubblicana:* Republican National Guard, Fascist force with internal police and military duties, 1943-1945

***Guardia di Finanza*:** Finance Guards, militarised finance and customs police force

MI6 The foreign intelligence service of the United Kingdom, also known as SIS

NARA National Archives and Records Administration, United States

No. 1 Intelligence Unit Cover name for the Italian SIS base.

No. 1 Special Force Cover name for SOE in Italy

OSS Office of Strategic Services, the United States intelligence agency during the Second World War

OVRA *Organizzazione per la vigilanza e la repressione dell' antifascismo:* Organisation for Vigilance and Repression of Anti-Fascism, Fascist secret police

PCI *Partito comunista italiano:* Italian Communist Party

RSI *Repubblica sociale italiana:* The Italian Social Republic of Mussolini, 1943-1945

SD *Sicherheitsdienst:* German security service

SI Secret Intelligence Branch of the OSS

SIS Secret Intelligence Service, also known as MI6. The foreign intelligence service of the United Kingdom

SO Special Operations Branch of the OSS

SOE Special Operations Executive: British secret service 'for subversion and sabotage against the enemy overseas'

SS *Schutzstaffel:* German elite corps of the Nazi Party with police and military powers

TNA The National Archives, United Kingdom

WO War Office, United Kingdom

ABOUT THE AUTHOR

Anglo-Italian historian MALCOLM TUDOR is a graduate of the University of Wales and lives in the principality. His British father was a soldier with the Eighth Army in Italy and his Italian mother and grandparents helped many escaped British and Allied prisoners of war in their home and in the mountains. The author has written ten books on Italy during the Second World War and has a specialised knowledge of the secret war behind enemy lines. He has interviewed veterans, visited the scenes of their operations, and conducted international research.

ACKNOWLEDGEMENTS

After more than 10 years of visiting Milan and the Italian lakes to establish facts and to reach conclusions there are many reasons to thank numerous Italian citizens. I'm also indebted to the former servicemen and partisans of different nations who have provided me with information and to the archivists of the official records that record their heroic deeds. The insights that I have gained are all set out in this book. Finally, as usual, I would like to thank family and friends for their help and advice.

AUTHOR'S NOTE

Between the 18th and 28th of April 1945, Benito Mussolini made his last ever journey, from Gargnano to Giulino di Mezzegra, from life to death.

How did he really die? Was it simply an execution by Italian partisans or were foreign secret agents involved?

Mussolini was captured in Dongo on Lake Como on 27 April while trying to escape disguised as a German serviceman and was shot next day together with his lover, Claretta Petacci. In the late afternoon, sixteen of his most loyal supporters also paid with their lives.

On the morning of the 29th, the bodies were dumped in a square in Milan and exposed to the fury of a mob. Mussolini, Petacci, and five others were finally hoisted onto the gantry of a petrol station and hung upside down.

The Fascist leader had been the Prime Minister of the Kingdom of Italy from October 1922 until July 1943, when he was overthrown in a palace coup and finally imprisoned in a ski resort hotel. In September, he re-emerged to lead the puppet Italian Social Republic following a spectacular rescue by German forces.

However, Mussolini had lost most of his popular support by 1945. In the third week of April, the partisans were about to launch the final rising and Allied forces were advancing on the heels of the German Army, which was falling back through northern Italy to Switzerland and Austria.

Mussolini left Lake Garda together with his followers and German escort on 18 April and settled in the Milan Prefecture. A week later, they fled the city and took the road for Lake Como after the failure of talks to agree an 'honourable surrender' with leaders of the Resistance.

The British, Americans, and Italians then began a furious race to lay their hands on Mussolini, all with their own units and aims, some wanting him to face justice, some wanting to end his life.

What really happened next has been the subject of debate and speculation ever since.

The so-called 'official version' was immediately put forward by the Italian Communist Party. It claimed that a partisan known as Colonel Valerio had shot both Mussolini and Petacci in front of the gate of the Villa Belmonte in Giulino di Mezzegra at 4.10 p.m. on 28 April.

Some obvious inconsistencies in the account have led to the emergence of many alternative theories over the years, especially once the remaining major participants in the story were no longer around to contradict them.

These versions usually claim that the couple did not die in the afternoon or even outside the Villa Belmonte. Instead, it is said to have taken place during the morning in or near the house where they spent their last night and at the hands of people other than the mysterious Colonel Valerio.

The stories also often highlight the participation of foreign secret agents, especially those of the British Special Operations Executive (SOE), with the suggestion that they wanted to retrieve compromising secret letters between Winston Churchill and Mussolini.[1]

As the new Prime Minister, Churchill did write to Mussolini on 16 May 1940 in an attempt to keep Italy out of the war, but received a negative reply two days later. It is claimed that other letters were written later in the hostilities with the intention of creating a separate peace between the two nations, which would have led to the formation of an anti-soviet alliance.

As Mussolini is also often said to have been carrying his most precious documents with him at the time of his arrest and capture, it is suggested that they included the secret correspondence.

The theory then goes that Churchill decided to have the dictator killed by his agents in Italy to prevent him disclosing its existence during a public trial for war crimes.

Numerous secret agents from the Office of Strategic Services (OSS) of the United States also took part in the large-scale manhunt for Mussolini across the lakes and mountains.

What really happened? To strip away fact from fiction this book uses a variety of original sources. These include wartime secret intelligence reports from the United Kingdom and the United States, Italian records, and first-hand accounts of people involved in the drama.

We begin our investigation by following the wanderings of Mussolini's convoy on his final journey.

1 MUSSOLINI'S NIGHTMARE

Benito Mussolini left the Villa Feltrinelli in Gargnano on Lake Garda for the last time on the morning of 18 April 1945.

Before leaving, he went into a room where his youngest son, Romano, age seventeen, was playing a tune from Franz Lehár's famous operetta *The Merry Widow* on a piano.

The dictator had been given the original score as a gift by the elderly Hungarian composer and became emotional whenever he heard the music.

When Romano saw his father entering the room he thought that he wanted to listen to him for a few moments, looking over his shoulder as he had done many times before. Instead, he hugged him and said in a sad and low voice: 'Goodbye, Romano, continue to play.'

Mussolini went into the courtyard and climbed into a waiting car that would take him to Milan. He told his wife, Rachele, 'I will return in two or three days at the most,' which, he said, was the time required to discover if it was still possible to halt the Allied advance.

She replied: 'Come back as soon as you can, but please telephone at least once a day.'

Romano went to the window and saw that as the car was starting up his father gave him one last wave. He would never return, though his family all believed that he could have tried to save himself at any time.

However, Mussolini never showed any interest in escaping, once saying: 'I do not want to beg for salvation while the majority sacrifice themselves for me and the dignity of Italy.'

He lived by instinct and emotion and still had not completely abandoned hope, though everything seemed to be collapsing around him. He had told Rachele in February 1945: 'Hitler accompanied me in person to the factories in Germany where weapons were being prepared that will change the outcome of the war. The important thing is not to lose trust.'

This was also the theme of Mussolini's only public speech as head of the Italian Social Republic, made during his previous visit to Milan on 16 December 1944, when he had spoken to an excited crowd of devoted followers in the Lirico Theatre.

Rachele recalled that on the one hand her husband was aware that the war was lost. The great cities of the north were battered by Allied bombing and from time to time fighter planes roared overhead in search of tempting targets to machine gun on the ground. Now the Italian military apparatus was crumbling and the Allied final offensive was under way. The American 10th Mountain Division breached German positions around Bologna and advanced rapidly up the Via Emilia, while the 8th Army pushed through the Argenta Gap south of Ferrara and broke into the Po Valley.

On the other hand, Mussolini was also a hopeless dreamer. He had always thought that he could reach the Valtellina, the River Adda valley that runs along the foothills of the Alps, and organise resistance with his most trusted men (whom, he was assured, would number in the thousands). Evoking the ancient Spartans, he boasted: 'It will be the Thermopylae of Fascism. Like Leonidas and his heroes, I will sacrifice myself to bar the pass to the enemy.'

For this force to reach the valley unmolested his eldest son, Vittorio, had proposed a plan of action to Cardinal Ildefonso Schuster of Milan, who had been in contact with both the Germans and the Allies for some time in an attempt to avoid bloodshed and destruction in the city. Benito told Rachele: 'Schuster is a great negotiator, I have confidence in him.' The Cardinal's Secretary, Don Giuseppe Bicchierai, discussed the possibility of some form of negotiated settlement with Allen Dulles, American OSS station head in Switzerland, but the reply was negative. The Allies demanded the unconditional surrender of the Fascists and were not inclined to give them safe conduct, still less to the Valtellina, which would have led to new conflicts and a lengthening of the war.

Mussolini was very disappointed, as the refusal added to a nightmare that had haunted him for months: the prospect of capture and trial by the Americans. On one of the last occasions when he dined with the family at Villa Feltrinelli he told them: 'I already foresee the trial I will receive in Madison Square, with the people on the stands looking at me as if I was a captured beast. It would be better to die with weapons in hand; only this would be the worthy conclusion of my existence.'

He arrived in Milan at around 8 p.m. on 18 April in his Alfa Romeo 2500, followed by a train of ministers and officials and by his young lover, Claretta Petacci, who went to stay with her parents and sister in the city centre. Since November 1943 she had lived at Gardone, a short distance away from Mussolini's Villa Feltrinelli on Lake Garda. He began seeing her again every so often in sad and furtive meetings.

She was accompanied to Milan by her brother, Marcello, who was hated by the entire Fascist leadership because of the privileged position he enjoyed owing to his sister and to the ruthless way in which he exploited it. Claretta's parents and sister were preparing to leave Italy on forged passports, and she told them: 'Half of my heart will go with you to Spain, but the rest of me belongs to the *Duce*. I must go wherever he goes.' The trio flew safely from Malpensa airport to Barcelona in a German aircraft on 23 April.

The Fascists installed themselves in the Prefecture in Corso Monforte. Every day, Mussolini held anxious discussions with his closest collaborators. It was a time for hard decisions: whether to surrender (and if so, to the Allies or to the Resistance), whether to attempt escape to a neutral country, or, finally, whether to fight pending an 'honourable surrender' after taking refuge with the most trusted men in the fabled redoubt of the Valtellina.

As soon as he arrived in the city, Mussolini made plans to attend a service in the cathedral to honour fallen servicemen and to speak to the people in the Lirico Theatre again. But on the morning of 20 April he learned that the fall of Bologna to the Anglo-Americans was imminent. That evening, 'tired, sad, and preoccupied as never before,' according to the journalist Ermanno Amicucci, he took comfort in watching a film of his December 1944 speech at the theatre, when his supporters' flame of devotion had been briefly rekindled.

A crowd of people were attracted to the Prefecture: ministers, soldiers, journalists, and the party faithful invaded the steps, the anterooms, and even Mussolini's office. He got angry from time to time, chasing everyone out and returning to sifting through the newspapers, writing a final article, or reading books of Greek philosophy and romantic poems.

The last loyalists described him as active as usual, lucidly sitting at his desk or talking with a group of ministers, but even they could not ignore the frequent incoherence of orders and opinions, which they justified by his lack of food and sleep. On the other hand, others who described him as hesitant, listless, or deluded, and always tired and depressed, were more believable.

Despite Mussolini's promise to constantly keep in touch with his family by telephone, they had to wait until 23 April to hear from him, a dark and humid day, when his German doctor, Professor Georg Zachariae (whom Hitler had placed in his villa in October 1943) observed in his diary that his patient was lower in morale than usual.

Seemingly, he had now decided to abandon everything, even his devoted comrades. 'I'll be with you tonight,' he told Rachele. But an hour later he had changed his mind and called again to let her know that he could not come, saying that Mantua had been occupied by the Allies and the roads leading to Brescia had been blocked. He concluded: 'Have patience and don't lose confidence; also, tell the children that we'll see one another soon.'

Rachele angrily interrupted him and said that it was not true that the roads were blocked, as a lorry carrying troops had just arrived from Milan without meeting any difficulty, and that once again he had been misinformed. Benito told her that she must leave immediately with the children (Romano and younger daughter, Anna Maria, age sixteen) for the Royal Villa in Monza, where he would join them. They arrived there at dawn and he telephoned three times, on the last occasion saying that he had arranged for his private secretary, Luigi Gatti, to accompany them to Como, where the secluded Villa Mantero, belonging to a silk industrialist, would be at their disposition.

Mussolini spent the day of the 24th addressing anyone who wanted to listen in a flat, subdued voice, as if he had given up hope, repeating the words he had spoken to a parade of militia in Brescia on 23 March: 'If the country is lost, it is pointless living.'

Elsewhere in the city, industrialist Gian Riccardo Cella, who had just bought the newspaper the *Popolo d'Italia* from Mussolini, met Christian Democrat lawyer Achille Marazza of the National Liberation Committee for Upper Italy and told him that the dictator wanted to meet their military commander, General Raffaele Cadorna.

Marazza replied that such a meeting was possible, but that above all Mussolini would have to negotiate with the Liberation Committee, as it was the only body able to deal with political matters.

This made a solution acceptable to the dictator far less likely, as they were split evenly between those who wanted him alive at all costs and those who were just as determined to see him dead.

2 FACING HIS ENEMIES

On the early evening of 25 April, Benito Mussolini met his mortal enemies under the mediation of Cardinal Ildefonso Schuster, Metropolitan Archbishop of Milan since 1929 and at age sixty-five his senior by four years.

Earlier in the day, the National Liberation Committee had announced the general rising and decreed that unspecified leading Fascists would be subjected to trial and punishment. Around three in the afternoon, Committee member Achille Marazza of the Christian Democrats called at the palace in Via Fontana to find out from Schuster's Secretary, Monsignor Giuseppe Bicchierai, how secret negotiations with the Germans were progressing. Suddenly, the Cardinal emerged from his room in an agitated state and announced that Mussolini would be arriving in 15 minutes. He lent Marazza his car with instructions to find General Cadorna and to bring him to the palace as soon as possible.

Mussolini arrived on time, together with the industrialist Gian Riccardo Cella; Prefect, Mario Bassi; Minister of the Interior, Paolo Zerbino; Under-Secretary to the Presidency of the Council, Francesco Barracu; and SS Second-Lieutenant Fritz Birzer, the head of the German bodyguard. They were joined shortly afterwards by Marshal Rodolfo Graziani, the Minister of National Defence and commander of Army Group Liguria.

The Cardinal recalled that Mussolini entered the audience room with a very sad face, which gave him an impression of a man almost benumbed by immense misfortune. They sat down on a pink, plush divan positioned against the wall facing the door. The room was austere, with high ceilings, antique furniture, classical paintings, and red damask on the walls.

To lift Mussolini's spirits, Schuster reminded him of the fall of Napoleon. He seemed to like the comparison and replied: 'My empire of one hundred days is also about to expire. Like Bonaparte, I must meet my destiny with resignation.' The conversation languished and he seemed very tired. The Cardinal asked him if he had read a book that he had written, *Saint Benedict and his Times*, and, when he said that he had not, gave him a copy and recommended him to keep it, saying that it would comfort him in the future.

Seeing Mussolini so depressed, Schuster persuaded him to accept a small glass of rosolio liqueur and a biscuit. With a remorseful voice, the dictator confided that when he was a prisoner on the island of Maddalena in the summer of 1943 a priest had offered to help him to return to the Catholic faith; as a result, he had decided to attend Holy Mass, but on that very day had been sent back to the mainland. The Cardinal urged him to consider his Calvary as the atonement for his sins before a just and merciful God. Mussolini was moved, squeezing his hand in devotion and almost seeming about to cry.

He continued to touch on a variety of topics, but without enthusiasm and in a subdued voice, like 'a man without free will,' recalled Schuster, 'as if listlessly accepting his fate.'

He asked Mussolini what he intended to do and he replied that on the following day the army and the militia would be dissolved and he would withdraw to the Valtellina with three thousand Blackshirts. The Cardinal replied that the likely number would be a tenth of that, and Mussolini said: 'Perhaps a few more, not many though, I have no illusions.'

'And so, do you intend to continue the war in the mountains?'

'For a short period,' he replied, smiling nervously, 'and then I will surrender.'

Marazza had difficulty in finding General Cadorna and so it was around six in the evening when they finally arrived at the palace, accompanied by engineer Riccardo Lombardi from the Action Party and by lawyer Giustino Arpesani of the Liberal Party. Communist and Socialist members of the Liberation Committee were absent from the little delegation.

The newcomers were taken into the audience room, where the Cardinal and Mussolini had waited for almost three hours. Schuster came to greet them cordially and the dictator rose from the divan with an air that to Marazza seemed strangely deferential. The lawyer introduced the other partisans to the Cardinal and in his turn he made a gesture as if to present Mussolini, who held out his hand clumsily to each of them. They touched it uneasily and Marazza noted that his face was ashen and strained and that he was wearing a shabby and crumpled militia uniform and dusty and baggy boots.

Schuster and Mussolini returned to the divan, and the members of the Liberation Committee sat opposite them in silk armchairs on the other side of an oval table of white marble.

After an embarrassing silence, Mussolini turned towards Cadorna, who immediately gestured that he should speak to Marazza.

In a very polite tone the dictator asked: 'Well then, lawyer, what have you got to say to me?'

'The instructions I received are rigorous and I have nothing more to ask of you than to surrender unconditionally.'

Mussolini immediately stiffened and murmured: 'I haven't come here for this. I've been deceived.'

Marazza asked: 'What have you been told?'

'That the families of the leaders could gather at Varese and that the soldiers would be concentrated in the Valtellina…'

'These are simply details, which we are willing to negotiate once unconditional surrender is accepted,' Marazza replied.

'Well then we can continue the discussion,' responded Mussolini in a friendly tone. Marazza recalled that he had a strange forced smile, almost as if he wanted to attract sympathy. It was agreed that the Fascist armed forces and militia would be treated as prisoners of war and that their families would be safeguarded, though the leaders would be tried. No one asked for details.

Marshal Graziani entered the room and as soon as Mussolini had spoken he got to his feet, with his chest puffed out as if addressing his troops in the barracks, and began a long speech insisting that it would be wrong to begin surrender negotiations without first consulting their German ally. He concluded: 'It would be disloyal on our part; we have always been on the side of fidelity and honour, or so I have believed.' Mussolini looked irritated.

Marazza turned to the Marshal and said calmly: 'Perhaps the Government of the Social Republic and its Minister of War do not know that the Germans have been negotiating the surrender with us for more than ten days.' [1]

Mussolini seemed as if he had been hit by an electric current and turned angrily to Schuster, sitting alongside him on the divan, and demanded an explanation. He admitted that Marazza's disclosure was true and that SS General Karl Wolff had been negotiating with him through the German Consul and SS Colonel Walter Rauff. At that moment, Don Bicchierai entered the room and announced: 'The Germans have confirmed that they agree to surrender, but have not yet signed, promising to do so within 24 hours.'

Mussolini jumped up indignantly and yelled: 'The Germans have always treated us as slaves and now they've betrayed us.'

He continued in this vein for a long time, listing offences suffered and humiliations endured, and concluded by saying that he felt released from every obligation to the Germans and would resume his liberty of action, going immediately to reproach the Consul and then making a proclamation on the radio.

Marazza interrupted him, saying that it was getting late and that there was no time to lose, as Fascists and partisans were already fighting on the outskirts of Milan.

Mussolini glanced at his wristwatch and said: 'I'm going to see the Germans. I will be back in an hour.' After another token handshake, he picked up the book given to him by the Cardinal, who accompanied him to the anteroom and tried to persuade him not to go to see the Germans or to speak on the radio, saying that these moves would ruin everything. Mussolini did not reply and barely acknowledged Schuster's farewell.

As the Fascists went down the steps of the palace they crossed paths with another group coming up. The firebrand Secretary of the Socialist Party for Upper Italy, Sandro Pertini, had abruptly ended a workers' rally at the Borletti precision instruments factory as soon as he heard of the meeting and driven like a madman through the streets to get to the palace. He was accompanied by a Communist member of the Liberation Committee, Emilio Sereni. As they were hurrying up the steps, they paid no attention to the men who were coming down and so did not recognise Mussolini among them.

Following his departure, the members of the Committee sat and waited for his return. After some time the former Prefect of Milan, Carlo Tiengo, a suave lawyer, joined them in the audience room; he turned to General Cadorna and said that he was commanded by General Filippo Diamanti to offer the surrender of the Fascist garrison.

Marazza intervened and said: 'Do as you wish, we've more important matters to consider.'

Pertini then shouted at his colleagues that they should have arrested Mussolini and that even if he surrendered, he would only be held for two or three days and then be brought to trial. They replied: 'You're dreaming, we'll hand him over to the Allies as agreed.' At that point Marazza realised that Tiengo, who had heard everything, had slipped out of the room. In his rapidly emptying audience room, Cardinal Schuster anxiously asked Pertini: 'Whatever is going to happen now?' Your Eminence,' he replied, 'the wheel started turning this morning, no one can stop it now.'

Mussolini's German doctor, Georg Zachariae, described him 'as pale as death, with his face extremely drawn' when he returned to the Prefecture. Climbing the steps two at a time and meeting Fascist journalist Asvero Gravelli, he told him: 'You know what the Cardinal said to me: 'Repent your sins!' He shouted at the industrialist Gian Riccardo Cella: 'You have deceived me and led me into a trap!' To another person, he said: 'We have been betrayed by the Germans and by the Italians.' Finally, he came face to face with General Heinz Wening, commander of the German garrison, a man half a metre taller than himself, who knew nothing of the secret negotiations going on with the Allies. Swearing and shaking his fist in his face, the dictator shouted that the Germans were all unfair and treacherous. The General did not react, standing to attention and remaining silent.

But then Mussolini's fury was spent and he fell back into an inert listlessness, unable to meet the demands of the shocked mob of people around him, some asking for orders, some giving advice, some wanting to remain, some wanting to leave.

The chaos was interrupted by the dramatic arrival of the former prefect Carlo Tiengo, who was breathless after running from the Archbishop's palace to report the threat by Sandro Pertini that even if Mussolini surrendered to the Liberation Committee he would be handed over to a people's tribunal, which would inevitably lead to revolutionary justice and death.

The dictator, who had been limply resisting the insistence of hardliners that there should be no surrender, immediately shouted that his enemies wanted to have another 25 July, referring to the day in 1943 when he was overthrown in a palace coup, thundering: 'They will not succeed.'

He then gave the order: 'We leave immediately for Como.'

3 FASCISTS IN FLIGHT

After suddenly deciding to flee Milan on the evening of 25 April, Mussolini went down to the courtyard of the Prefecture and with difficulty men of the Black Brigades created a path for him through the milling crowd of people. With a machine gun on his shoulder, he climbed heavily into his Alfa Romeo 2500, sitting alongside his close friend Nicola Bombacci with a suitcase on his knee.

Mussolini's German bodyguard of thirty men were told that he intended to visit Italian troops about to be sent to the front. Commander of the squad, Waffen SS *Untersturmführer* (Second-Lieutenant) Fritz Birzer, had orders from General Karl Wolff to follow and protect Mussolini, but also to prevent him escaping to a neutral country. Birzer, aged 41, from Munich, and a veteran of the Russian front, had arrived in Italy in January with the anti-aircraft unit *3-II Flak Einheit* of the Panzer Grenadier Division SS *Reichsführer*, an armoured infantry formation created in 1943 from elements of the police and the personal guard of Heinrich Himmler.

The escort also included two car loads of men in plain clothes belonging to the *Sicherheitsdienst (SD),* the secret security service, which included espionage and often sabotage in its scope. The detachment, whose job was to watch Mussolini and report his movements and actions to their head office in Berlin, was led by forty-eight-year-old *Hauptsturmführer* (Captain) Otto Kisnat.

However, Birzer recalled: 'My decisions in following Mussolini were autonomous and I made them on my personal and complete responsibility.' Kisnat also left the convoy to return to Gargnano to close down his office, only reappearing on the afternoon of the 26th.

It had gone seven when Mussolini's convoy drove out of the Prefecture. Birzer placed his *Kübelwagen* (the German equivalent of a jeep) in front of the dictator's Alfa Romeo and they were followed by a lorry full of SS troops, the two car loads of Kisnat's SD men, and about thirty luxurious cars carrying ministers, party officials, and their families. One of the ministers asked another: 'Where are we going?' 'God knows,' his companion replied, 'perhaps to our deaths.' Also in the convoy were Claretta Petacci and her brother Marcello and his family.

Towards nine in the evening, a weary Mussolini arrived at the Como Prefecture in Via Volta, where he found the same confusion as in Milan: a crowd of the lost, irresolute, and fearful. It took an hour for the Prefect, Renato Celio, to be found and to return to the headquarters. Various ministers gradually arrived with their wives and families, as well as senior officers from the army and militia.

The dark evening was broken by a fleeting visit to the dictator by Claretta Petacci, who had found accommodation nearby in the Albergo Firenze.

Mussolini asked several times if the truck he was expecting had arrived. He was carrying some of his most important documents with him, but the rest had been taken from a secret hiding place in Gargnano and loaded onto a Fiat Balilla pickup truck in two zinc military boxes for consignment to Como, presumably to help him in any future trial. According to Romano Mussolini, the driver was accompanied by a secret agent and by Maria Righini, a maid from the Romagna, who had been in the service of the family of his late brother Bruno for many years.

However, the truck broke down at Garbagnate, north-west of Milan, and had to be pushed into a farmyard. Righini managed to hitch a lift to the Prefecture and to tell Mussolini what had happened.

He immediately sent agents in three cars to recover the vehicle and documents, but by the time they arrived they had already fallen into the hands of partisans of the 16th Brigade led by the Allievi brothers.

Birzer managed to telephone the German Consulate in Milan,

fearing that Mussolini (codenamed Karl Heinz) intended to try to escape to Switzerland, and he was told by one of Ambassador Rahn's staff that everyone had left and that he was to act as he saw fit, adding: 'If Karl Heinz attempts to flee, kill him!'

Following the telephone conversation, Birzer went to the commander of the German military garrison and told him of his fears that Mussolini wanted to escape. The Captain replied that they had sixty men between them, which was a force more than capable of taking him prisoner.

Birzer returned to the Prefecture and soon afterwards saw the same officer arrive at the request of Marshal Graziani, who had asked him for information about the deployment of guards along the Swiss border. While going down the stairs after the meeting, the Captain told Birzer that the Italians wanted to escape, but that he had given them the wrong directions.

Former Interior Minister Guido Buffarini-Guidi arrived at the Prefecture and tried to persuade Mussolini to make the attempt, saying that he knew all the crossings and smugglers' paths. But the dictator still believed in the boastful claims of Alessandro Pavolini, founder and commander of the Black Brigades, who had promised to bring thousands of armed men from Milan, and therefore decided to wait.

Paolo Porta, Federal Commissar of Como and commander of the XI Black Brigade Cesare Rodini, said he was certain of the loyalty of his unit and that it was strong enough to defend Mussolini if deployed to the zone of Cadenabbia, where it would be easier to mount a strong resistance.

The Commissar, a chain-smoking fanatic, had waged war on the partisans for many months from his headquarters at the Casa del Fascio, a futuristic building by Terragni with a glass atrium, and from the barracks of his brigade alongside the Como Borghi station.

Immediately, Mussolini exclaimed with sudden enthusiasm: 'I will go to the mountains with Porta. Surely, five hundred men can be found who will follow me.'

After supper, he asked about Rachele, Romano, and Anna Maria, who were now staying nearby at the secluded Villa Mantero. At two in the morning he sent them a hasty farewell letter, which Rachele committed to memory and made the children do the same before destroying it:

Dear Rachele,

I have come to the last phase in my life, the last page in my book. Perhaps we two will not see one another again; that is why I am writing and sending you this letter. I ask forgiveness for all the wrong which involuntarily I have done to you. But you know that for me you have been the only woman that I have truly loved. I swear this to you before God and before Bruno at this supreme moment. You know that we must go to the Valtellina. You must try to get to the Swiss frontier with the children. There, you will make a new life. I think they will not refuse you entry because I have helped them in every way and you have nothing to do with politics. If this should fail, you must give yourself up to the Allies, who perhaps will be more generous than the Italians. I commend Anna and Romano to you, particularly Anna, who has most need of your care. You know how much I love them. Bruno, from the sky, will help us. I kiss and embrace you, together with the children.

Your Benito

Bruno was the couple's airman son. He had been killed at age twenty-three in a crash on 7 August 1941 while testing an experimental Piaggio P 108 bomber.

After reading the letter, Rachele felt the urgent need to speak to her husband on the telephone. She got through to the Prefecture and asked him: 'How are you? What do you intend to do? Who is with you?'

Rather theatrically, he replied: 'There's no longer anyone, I'm alone, Rachele, and I see that everything is finished.'

'But, your personal guard, your soldiers...'

'I don't know. They have not arrived yet. I don't even see Cesarotti, my driver anymore; he must have gone too. You were right when you told me not to trust him.'

Rachele recalled: 'Benito's voice was sad and it stayed in my memory like an anguished echo. It seemed impossible to believe that everything was ending in this way; he was setting out alone towards his destiny and I was not able to be with him. It was only left for to me to follow the advice of my husband and to reach Switzerland with my children before it was too late.'

Tired of waiting for the Blackshirts to arrive, Mussolini decided to move farther up the lakeside. At 4.40 in the morning, a German sentry saw him coming down the steps of the Prefecture. Birzer, hearing the guard shout, 'Karl Heinz is escaping,' ran to his vehicle and drove it across the entrance.

'*Duce*, you can't go away without telling your escort.'

'Get out of the way. I can do what I want and go wherever I want. Clear the exit!'

Birzer called to his troops: 'Get ready. Load your weapons and prepare the hand grenades. Five men, follow me!' He pointed his machine gun and advanced towards Mussolini, saying: 'Now you can leave.'

The dictator gave in and his party meekly followed the German vehicles out of the courtyard.

It was raining by the time they arrived at Menaggio, a small lakeside holiday resort where many evacuees and public bodies had taken shelter. At 5.30 a.m. Mussolini stopped his Alfa Romeo in front of a school on the main road, which was being used as a Blackshirt barracks. After pacing up and down for a few minutes, he walked a hundred metres to the elegant terraced house of Emilio Castelli, Vice-Commissar of Como and Commander of the VI Company of the local XI Black Brigade Cesare Rodini. Mussolini lay down in a ground floor bedroom and tried to sleep as the other vehicles in the convoy came to a halt.

Luigi Gatti, the dictator's private secretary, afraid that such a large concentration would arouse suspicion and be reported to the Communist partisans, ordered most of the drivers to go back down the road about five kilometres to Cadenabbia. They reluctantly agreed and did so.

After resting for three hours, Mussolini came out and gave orders for the other cars to follow him inland to Grandola, high up in the mountains overlooking the lake. Birzer had a job keeping the vehicles in sight as they ascended the steep, winding road. Outside Grandola, they turned sharp left and raced up a narrow track to the four-storey Miravalle Hotel, which had been requisitioned by a detachment of Finance Guards.

By afternoon, the drive and forecourt of the hotel were packed with vehicles and the rooms were full of Fascists, now extremely worried about the non-arrival of Pavolini and the Blackshirt reinforcements.

However, Castelli gave the dictator a reassuring view of the local situation, saying that the zone was quiet as a result of successful roundups against the partisans over recent months.

Rather inconveniently, at that very moment the Prefect of Novara, Enrico Vezzalini, turned up with his head bandaged after being wounded in an attack by rebels near Como. He swore that 'thousands of trustworthy youths are ready to fight to the death' in Mussolini's defence (but did not say where they were).

The dictator also heard that Rachele and the children had failed in their escape attempt. At three in the morning a black Lancia picked them up from the Villa Mantero and took them to the Swiss frontier at Ponte Chiasso. Rachele got out of the car and asked the guards to let them enter the country.

One of them disappeared to make a telephone call and then, shaking his head, said that he had spoken to Bern and had received the order not to let them pass. The family learned later that there had been no communication with the capital; evidently the refusal was due to the fear of getting into trouble for letting Mussolini's wife and two of their children enter the country. But by now Benito's family had gone out of his life and he did not seek any other news or write any more letters.

Sitting at the end of the table was a beautiful, blonde young girl in the uniform of the auxiliaries, with a white shirt, black scarf, and a belt. She was Elena Curti Cucciati, his natural daughter from a liaison with one his favourite mistresses, Angela Curti Cucciati. The girl had worked as a secretary in the Ministry of Popular Culture at Maderno and every few days would visit Gargnano to read the newspapers with him and to repeat the gossip she had heard round and about.

Elena had left Milan in a small convoy of vehicles assembled by Pavolini. When they reached Como they found that Mussolini had already left, but caught up with him at the Castelli house in Menaggio. Pavolini then returned to Como in an attempt to drum up more support from his Blackshirts, while Elena went on to join the others at the Hotel Miravalle.

Rumours surrounding her paternity did not go down at all well with Claretta Petacci, who got it into her head that this was a new lover who had come to replace her. Claretta followed Mussolini into a room and began shouting at him in a fit of jealously, so loudly that he ran to close the window so that people would not hear, and as he turned, slipped, stumbled on a carpet, fell down heavily and got up with a large bruise on his cheekbone. Someone recounted that as he emerged from the room, he snapped: 'Take her away! Women are better left at home in circumstances like these.'[1]

Perhaps to clear the air, Elena volunteered to return to Como to trace the missing Pavolini. To avoid being stopped by partisans she went on a bicycle and after an exhausting journey was able to find him in the Fascist Federation building. She passed on the message that Mussolini was desperately awaiting him in Menaggio and he leapt into an armoured car and was driven off, leaving her to cycle back alone. After an hour, she caught up with them at Argegno and was at last allowed to climb on board the vehicle on its journey to Menaggio.

Back at the hotel in Grandola, at around 4 p.m., former Interior Minister, Guido Buffarini-Guidi, and the Minister of Industrial Production and the Corporate Economy, Angelo Tarchi, left in an attempt to cross the Swiss border.

However, the two cars carrying them were stopped at a roadblock in San Pietro Sovera by Finance Guards and partisans from Porlezza. Buffarini-Guidi claimed to be a lawyer called Alfredo Cignani, though Tarchi admitted to his real identity. They were accompanied by four public security agents.

The former minister had a false passport provided by the Varese Police Headquarters three days earlier, but when the photograph was examined he was recognised. Both of the men were carrying large amounts of Italian Lire, Spanish Pesetas, and Canadian and American Dollars. Buffarini-Guidi also had lists of significant quantities of fabrics belonging to him at various companies in Gallarate Varese. The pair were handed over to the National Liberation Committee of Porlezza. Buffarini-Guidi was shot in Milan on 10 July 1945, while Tarchi was passed on to the Allies, tried by the Italians for 'collaboration with the German invader,' and finally amnestied.

The four security agents were held briefly and then allowed to return to their units, while the driver managed to run back to the Hotel Miravalle and to announce the capture of all the others.

Birzer had always suspected that Mussolini intended to escape to Switzerland, as they had not followed the most direct route to the Valtellina along the eastern shore of the lake, and this belief was strengthened when he had tried to leave Como without his knowledge at 4.40 a.m. on 26 April.

The former Lieutenant recalled: 'Why did he want to leave without his German escort, which he had often praised? And everyone knows that I prevented it with the raised machine guns of my men.'

Mussolini had then abandoned the lakeside road for the Hotel Miravalle at Grandola, a few kilometres from Switzerland, and sent Buffarini-Guidi and Tarchi to the border. It was only on the return to Menaggio on the evening of 26 April that Mussolini said to him: 'Birzer, tell your men to get ready, we're leaving immediately for Merano.'

In the meantime, he had asked him to go with his SS force to liberate the pair. In reply, he suggested that they should be accompanied by the captives' driver, who knew the route to follow. However, the man said that he was tired out, asked for a little time to rest, and was never seen again. So Birzer did not go to San Pietro Sovera.

Kisnat was even more explicit on Mussolini's intentions. In a statement in 1968, he recalled that at the Hotel Miravalle in Grandola he had told him: 'I sent them to negotiate with the border authorities over the possibility of crossing into Switzerland with my followers, but this was no longer possible. We leave early tomorrow for Merano.'

Around 8 p.m., Mussolini had told Birzer: 'We are moving north to Merano. We shall move at once.'

The Lieutenant replied: 'My men have been on duty almost without a rest for the past 36 hours and they have had only one meal; I must insist they be allowed a night's rest.'

Mussolini frowned with surprise and then said in a low voice: 'Very well, if you wish. We shall delay until five in the morning.'

If he had left immediately, he could probably have made a detour to Chiavenna along roads still manned by the Germans and cleared of partisans, perhaps in time to fly from a small airfield where a Fiat BR.20 Cicogna bomber was held in readiness according to a plan of escape advanced by his son Vittorio.

But if the men of Birzer were tired, he described Mussolini as undone by the lack of sleep, with eyes drawn and the look of a man who had completely lost the capacity to function.

As the Germans and Fascists settled down for the night in Menaggio, things were about to become ever more complicated.

4 THE LAKE PARTISANS

At around midnight, Lieutenant Birzer was suddenly woken up by an excited guard. 'There's another of our units here,' he said. 'They have just arrived in the town, several hundred men and a long convoy of trucks. I think they're *Luftwaffe*, sir, and I've brought the officer to see you.'

The man was tall and slender, with a tanned face and brown eyes, and wore the light blue uniform of the *Luftwaffe*, with brown collar tabs of a communications unit. Birzer recognised that he was a fellow south German by his speech.

He introduced himself as Lieutenant Hans Fallmeyer and said that his unit of one hundred and sixty men of the *Luftwaffe's* radar unit, the *Luftnachrichten-Regiment 200*, had been on the move for several days in thirty lorries.

On the previous day they had been held up several times by partisan units, but had been allowed to proceed once it became clear that their convoy only consisted of Germans leaving Italy to return home. 'They didn't appear very interested in us. I think they were really looking for Italians,' Fallmeyer concluded.

'Italians,' said Birzer gloomily, 'I'm surrounded by them. There's one in particular who would be most interesting to any partisans we met…'

Fallmeyer nodded. 'So I understand.'

'It's Mussolini, of course,' said Birzer.

'Yes, everyone seems to know that he's here.'

'Of course! I'm surprised the whole world doesn't know. We've been here all day and they've been running all over the countryside. Hopeless!'

Birzer asked 'What would you say if I suggested that we merge our units and move north together? We'll be safer that way, I think.'

'Certainly, anything you say,' Fallmeyer replied. 'But there is one thing. I don't really want to know anything about Mussolini. I want to get my men and myself back home with the minimum of trouble. Do you understand me?'

'I do. I will be responsible for him.'

It was agreed that Fallmeyer's *Luftwaffe* unit would follow Birzer and the Italians at a distance of about three hundred metres, with a German motorcyclist maintaining contact between the two sections of the column.

Birzer started organising his men at four in the morning. Taking the lead would be the Italian armoured car that had turned up from Como under the command of Pavolini. It was eight metres long, two metres wide, and four metres tall, but in reality was a simple Lancia 3Ro heavy truck that had been equipped with a mobile turret, a 20 mm canon, three heavy machine guns, and armour plating from the arsenal at Piacenza. There was no sign of the three thousand men Pavolini had promised.

Mussolini asked him: 'Where are the Blackshirts?'

Pavolini limply gestured that they were outside.

'How many?'

'Twelve.'

This signified the end of any hope for the dictator. The Black Brigades of Como had surrendered to the partisans.

Even so, seeing so many armed men in the combined convoy, Mussolini exclaimed: 'With two hundred Germans I can go to the top of the world.' In reality, he would not get very far with these men, as their only wish was to return home as soon as possible. At 5.30, Mussolini gave his last ever order as he got into his Alfa Romeo: 'We leave for Merano!'

The column set off along the lakeside road, accompanied by a car with diplomatic plates carrying Doctor Marcello Petacci, his family, and his sister, Claretta. Elena Curti Cucciati took a seat in the armoured car with Alessandro Pavolini; Colonel Francesco Barracu, the Under-Secretary to the Presidency of the Council; and Mussolini's friend Nicola Bombacci.

After an hour's journey the vehicle ground to a halt and Pavolini stepped out, gave the Roman salute to Mussolini, and said: '*Duce*, I have the duty to personally guarantee your safety. Please join me in the armoured car.' After obtaining Birzer's permission, Mussolini climbed on board, wearing the grey-green uniform of the Fascist militia, and was surprised and delighted to find that Elena was already there.

The armoured car continued to lead the convoy in a slow procession along the narrow lakeside road as the occupants anxiously scanned the horizon. With the passing of every hour without any sign of partisans they became ever more confident that deliverance could be at hand.

However, their fate would soon be sealed by a ragtag assortment of rebels a few kilometers ahead of their convoy under the command of a twenty-five-year-old nobleman lawyer.

Pier Luigi Bellini delle Stelle was born in Florence on 14 May 1920. After completing his legal studies, he contacted the Como partisans in June 1944 through his sister, Eleanora, who was a teacher in Gravedona, and set off immediately with three companions. After a long march they reached the mountains and were welcomed as brothers by the men of the Puecher detachment.

The Count became known as Pedro. Recalling the reasons that had brought him to the mountains, he said: 'The basis of all my reasoning had been the firm conviction that the legal government of Italy was that of Badoglio, and that Mussolini and his gang were usurpers whose tenure of power was solely due to German aid and ruthless repression.'

The partisan detachment had been formed in March on the slopes of Monte Berlinghera (1,930 metres), which overlooks the upper lake and in wartime provided three routes for German and Fascist materials. The rebels' bases were only 15 hours march from the Swiss border. Their role from these strategic points was to observe enemy movements, deny them freedom of transit, and safeguard industrial plant. The unit consisted of about seventy men divided into three platoons, but weapons, food, and equipment were lacking and further supplies were difficult to obtain. In addition, there were no roads and the villages were few and poor, with limited pasture and scattered chestnut trees.

The detachment's baptism of fire came in an attack on Fascists passing through the lakeside village of Gera Lario at the end of June. It proved to be a failure, and though the men were able to withdraw without any losses, the action led to two large-scale enemy roundups; the second in mid-August lasted for four days and was followed by losses and desertions in the partisan ranks.

By the beginning of September the unit was reduced to just thirty men and their commander, known as Giorgio, had been killed. However, at this moment of crisis, the detachment was completely reorganised by Michele Moretti (Pietro Gatti), the Political Commissar, and by Luigi Canali (Captain Neri) from the area command - two of the main actors in our story.

Moretti was born in Como on 26 March 1908 to a family of Socialists and in his youth was a noted footballer. He joined the clandestine Communist Party in the late 1930s and became a union activist at the paper mill where he worked. In 1944, Moretti was one of the principal organisers of strikes in the Como area. As a result, he was arrested by the Fascist police and sentenced to deportation to Germany, but managed to escape from a detention camp at Sesto San Giovanni before this happened.

Canali was born in Como on 16 March 1912. He left school at age fifteen and began work as a bookkeeper, moving to the Funicular Society of Como-Brunate in the following year. He continued to study by correspondence courses, read widely, and learned several languages, including English, French, and Esperanto. In 1935, Canali was called up for army service and sent to the Abyssinian front, where he became a sergeant and radio telegraphist in the 74th Company of Military Engineers, serving until July 1938. On 22 April 1936, he had written to a friend:

You want to make me into a hero come what may. We must be half a million men against half as many blacks who are poorly equipped and have no air force. They are dying by the tens of thousands. We are still writing casualty lists of our men by name because they are so few. And yet supposedly we are heroes. Personally, I feel I have made greater moral and material efforts in civilian life with no one telling me anything. Have I been lucky? Then there are 499,000 other lucky ones in East Africa!

Once back in Italy, Canali worked at the Como hydro-electric company and obtained his diploma as an accountant. On the outbreak of war, he was sent to the Russian front, where he served as a captain in the engineers. He returned with the final contingent on 26 July 1943 and two months later married Giovanna Martinelli, with whom he had a daughter, Luisella.

Canali joined the Communist Party and became its representative on the Como National Liberation Committee. In the spring of 1944, he helped found the Proletarian Front with four others and assumed the battle name of Captain Neri. When one of the group, was arrested and killed by the Fascists, he took command of the formation, which then became known as the 52nd Garibaldi Brigade Luigi Clerici after his friend.

Over the coming months, Canali would be promoted to important roles in the regional organisation of the Garibaldi Divisions. As well as reorganising the Puecher detachment in September 1944, he and Moretti gained the support of local people and youth auxiliaries. The unit was further strengthened by the arrival of a Finance Guards officer called Urbano Lazzaro (Bill). He was born at Quinto Vicentino in the Veneto on 4 November 1924 and like the Count was a monarchist. Lazzaro had left Chiavenna in May 1944 and crossed the border into Switzerland, where he was temporarily interned. Within three weeks of his arrival on Monte Berlinghera he disarmed three troops of the Sondrio Black Brigade, capturing one and injuring the other two, and went on to carry out many more daring acts.

The 52nd Garibaldi Brigade Luigi Clerici now had a clearly-defined role and sphere of action. Links were also established with the partisan leadership in Milan, but the problem of supplies was left for the unit commander to solve, which presented great difficulties owing to the poverty of the region and the fear of reprisals against civilians.

The Count recalled: 'No Allied air force ever dropped supplies to us, possibly because of the difficulty of the terrain, nor did we have at our disposal workshops, explosive factories, or ordnance depots. We soon had to learn to fall back on our own resources. But our morale was excellent.'

The detachment went on the offensive again, but this led to another massive enemy roundup in the middle of October. The unit was reduced to just eighteen men and their new commander, known as Tom, left them. Moretti briefly took over command.

On 13 November, the men received a visit from the Brigade Commander, Giovanni Amelotti (Sardo), and the Political Commissar, Enrico Caronti (Romolo), both of whom would be captured and shot at Christmas-time. The Count was made Detachment Commander, Lazzaro the Political Commissar, and Moretti the Vice-Commissar.

December passed fairly quietly in the mountains, but enemy activity intensified in the towns and cities on the plains. The Count's sister, Eleanora, was imprisoned in Como and later in Milan, and was subjected to almost continuous and exhausting interrogation for the sin of having a partisan brother.

At the end of January 1945 the brigade received news that the enemy was planning another big drive against them and decided to move to the small ski resort of Madesimo in the Chiavenna Valley. The men reached the village after an arduous march lasting a day and half across snow-covered mountains. They cut the telephone lines and collected food and winter clothing from local shops and hotels, but were forced to return to Monte Berlinghera after five days, as the Fascists were assembling a force of three hundred men to attack them.

Four of the partisans had already deserted, weary of the lack of food and shelter and the very hard life. Canali, who had carried out an inspection along the lake before being arrested in January, found that only scattered detachments of the brigade were still in existence, totalling just sixty-nine men. The headquarters had been wiped out at the end of the year and the Puecher detachment remained without orders or contact with any higher command until the end of March 1945.

But morale remained high. They formed a squad of the most determined and efficient men and, though their first action was a failure, over successive weeks they were constantly in action. After crossing to the eastern shore of the lake by boat, a small patrol led by Lazzaro blew up the power substation in Colico on 7 March, so disrupting the transit of war materials along the Sondrio-Lecco-Milan railway line.

Towards the end of the month, the detachment received a visit from the inspector of the Lombardy divisional headquarters, known as Angelo, who brought news of the appointment of the Count as Commander of the brigade. At the time, his detachment consisted of just twenty-two men. They received three Sten guns, a Bren gun, and ammunition and used them in an attack on Fascists at the Hotel Turismo in Gravedona, killing two officers of the border militia, and also capturing three revolvers and a French MAS-38 submachine gun that will re-appear in our story.

Enemy raids began to intensify, and, recalled the Count: 'We began to get seriously worried that the Fascists, angered at the trouble we were giving them, might be planning a massive assault on us once and for all. It did not occur to us that they might be trying to clear the area so as to leave open their line of retreat through the Valtellina and the Brenner.'

On 24 April, the Gramsci detachment of the brigade was suddenly attacked by Blackshirts stationed at Dongo and scattered after a sharp fight; four partisans were killed and several more were wounded. Shortly afterwards, the Fascists departed by boat, leaving a small German barracks in the town.

On the 25th, the Count went with some of his men to the Gravedona area after hearing of troop movements, and from a house on the mountainside belonging to one of their informants they witnessed the Fascist militia leaving the small fishing village of Domaso in two motor-boats. Towards evening, the Count accompanied Lazzaro to the nearby hamlet of Pozzolo and rendezvoused with another six of their men. They decided to go down to Domaso in the morning to get some tobacco, which they knew would be distributed on ration cards.

The Count recalled: 'We went to Domaso as planned almost as soon as it was daylight and as we walked along little did we realise that we were walking into the greatest adventure of our lives.'

5 THE FAMOUS ROADBLOCK

At seven on the morning of 26 April, Count Pier Luigi Bellini delle Stelle and his seven men went in a search of tobacco, little thinking that it would be their last journey from the mountains as partisans.

The Count posted two men at each end of the village of Domaso, while he went with another one into a tobacconist's shop to buy half the ration intended for the local people. Meanwhile, Urbano Lazzaro and another partisan did the same at a second shop.

The news of the arrival of the rebels spread rapidly and when they met up again in the square they were surrounded by a crowd of people who slapped them on the back and shouted that the war was over.

At this point, the partisans had received no orders and were in the dark regarding the latest military situation. So they asked what was going on and were propelled into an ice-cream shop that possessed a radio. With the villagers, they listened to a sensational communique: 'The Allies have crossed the River Po; the German Army is in retreat. The Allies are in Brescia and are converging on Milan, where insurrection has broken out and partisan units have occupied all the key points and most of the barracks.'

The Count and Lazzaro decided that if they acted decisively they might be able to take over the area, though there were only eight of them and they knew that even if they brought down the other twenty from the mountains and found a few volunteers from the town they would only number fifty, with no heavy or automatic weapons.

A letter was sent to the commanding officer of the National Guard Frontier Legion in Gravedona saying that if they surrendered with their arms before 9 p.m. they would be given safe conduct, but, if not, would be attacked in strength and shot to the last man. Moretti was ordered to bring the rest of the men and arms down from the mountains and they went on to occupy Sorico and then Gera Lario, whose Fascist garrison had been withdrawn over the previous few days. The local parish priest, Don Franco Gusmaroli, also agreed to carry a demand from the partisans for the surrender of legionaries of the Frontier Guards protecting the Ponte del Passo, a strategic three-arch girder bridge joining the banks of the River Mera at the northern tip of the lake.

Later in the morning, Brigadier Giorgio Buffelli of the Finance Guards, with whom the detachment had been in touch for some time, arrived in Domaso to report that the Germans in Dongo seemed determined to resist at any cost. However, he said that he would do his best to ensure that they surrendered and promised to return with further news.

In the afternoon, the partisans learned that their ultimatum to the Fascist garrison at Ponte del Passo had been a total success. The Count and Lazzaro drove in that direction and on the way they met the column of men who had surrendered and were being brought to Gera Lario, their first prisoners.

In contrast, the nearby German garrison at Nuova Olonio was refusing to surrender and responded to partisan requests with bursts of machine gun fire. The Count jumped into a lorry with fifteen men and two machine guns salvaged from the Ponte del Passo garrison and quickly drove to the village.

The Count walked firmly up to the main gate with Lazzaro, waved a white flag, and shouted: 'Open up. We want to talk.' After a few minutes a door opened and they were led to meet three German officers, one of whom acted as interpreter. They saluted one another and the partisans placed their weapons on the table. The Count told the Germans that they had come to demand their surrender, that the Allies were advancing rapidly, and that their countrymen had ceased all resistance. If they surrendered he would guarantee the safety of their lives and possessions, but, if not, they would be attacked and exterminated to the last man. Despite this, the German commanding officer, a small, frail man, replied that without orders from a higher command it was his duty to resist at all costs.

However, after a heated discussion that lasted 15 minutes the Germans finally decided to surrender. The commander took his revolver out of its holster and handed it over to the Count. They all saluted and shook hands and the Germans were congratulated on their wise decision.

The Count left a few men to take charge of the prisoners and went at full speed back to Domaso with the rest of the partisans. When they arrived in the village they were surrounded by an even larger crowd of people, who by now were even more excited. They reported that the Fascists in Gravedona had also surrendered and were now being held in the local school and town hall. The Count ensured that there were sufficient guards and as he went out into the street a German car drew up with two partisans on the running board. The occupants, three members of the German criminal police, had been arrested at a rebel roadblock; they were placed in detention alongside the Fascist prisoners.

At that moment, Moretti arrived with Swiss national Alois Hofmann, a good friend of the partisans (and reputedly an intelligence agent for his country), who lived with his family in Domaso. He readily agreed to go with them to act as interpreter to demand the surrender of the German garrison at Gravedona and said that he already knew the commanding officer. They requisitioned the German car and drove to the enemy headquarters in the Albergo Italia.

The discussions lasted for some time, as the commander was at first unwilling to hear any talk of surrender, but finally relented on condition that safe conduct was guaranteed for him and his men to Switzerland, where they would be interned. The partisans agreed to the demand, as weapons were their main interest and they lacked resources to hold many more prisoners. The surrender was concluded with a handshake. The German officer agreed to telephone his counterpart in the garrison at Dongo to tell him that they had surrendered and that he should do the same, but his advice was rejected. However, as night was falling, Buffelli arrived with the news that his own mission to the same unit had finally been successful and they were now willing to discuss terms.

Hofmann and the partisans drove to Dongo, passing several of their own patrols on the way. Buffelli led them to the barracks and after being recognised by a sentry introduced them to the German commanding officer, a tall, heavily-built man with a resolute, intelligent face.

Here too negotiations were lengthy as the Germans did not trust the partisans, fearing that they would be shot once they surrendered. However, Hofmann intervened and guaranteed the good faith of the rebels. The commander finally decided to surrender after his safety and that of his men was guaranteed. They handed over their weapons and equipment, which were loaded onto a cart and taken to the Customs House. The barracks was taken over by the partisans and eight men were left to guard the prisoners.

The Count recalled that they then established their 'most advanced roadblock, protected by two heavy machine guns and a crateful of hand grenades,' on a narrow bend about half way between Dongo and Musso in an area known as Puncett. On the left, the rock rises vertically from the edge of the road, while there is a small wall and a sheer drop into the waters of the lake on the right.

The road was barely wide enough for a single vehicle to pass and has now been by-passed by a tunnel bored through the solid rock to the left. The area has been described as one of the most picturesque parts of northern Italy.

To block the road a barrier was created 'out of wire entanglements, a tree trunk, and huge blocks of stones.'

The night was now well advanced and the Count felt that they could rest on the positions they had occupied until morning, when they could proceed southwards towards Menaggio and possibly even as far as Como. In the meantime, well-armed patrols were sent out for liaison and observation across the large area between the roadblock and their new base at Ponte del Passo in the north.

At about three in the morning of 27 April, the Count, Moretti, and Lazzaro sat down in Hofmann's house in Domaso to discuss the wider situation. All they knew was based upon a letter sent via courier from Lecco by Luigi Canali (Captain Neri), which reported that most of the left bank of the lake was being liberated, but that there were still pockets of enemy resistance.

After deciding on their next moves, Moretti left for Gravedona, while the Count and Lazzaro retired to their beds just before dawn. They lay down exhausted but were not to be left in peace for very long. Two hours later they were suddenly woken up with the news that the massive German convoy was advancing steadily towards them along the narrow lakeside road.

6 THE ENEMY CONVOY

Once Count Pier Luigi Bellini delle Stelle discovered that the large German convoy was bearing down on his tiny partisan detachment he immediately sent a message to his men at the advance roadblock to stop them at all costs and to keep them talking until he arrived. The other units were prepared for combat while the Count, Lazzaro, and Hofmann set off to try and negotiate if at all possible, as if the Germans tried to force the blockade everything would be lost.

The partisans picked up Moretti in Gravedona on the way and dropped off Lazzaro in Dongo to stiffen resistance there. The road to Musso climbs steeply for almost a kilometre and then runs level for two or three hundred metres before dropping down towards the village. An armoured car was halted about halfway along the level stretch.

Partisans on the roadblock had fired a warning burst from a machine gun into the air. This was answered by the armoured car with several shots from automatic weapons, which killed an old workman who was walking to Dongo across the fields. Immediately afterwards, someone in a car waved a white flag; two partisans approached and a German officer asked to speak to their commander.

The Count, Moretti, and Hofmann passed their roadblock and found a similar number of enemy officers waiting for them by the armoured car. The Count asked their commander, Lieutenant Hans Fallmeyer, who spoke Italian fairly well, what his intentions were. He replied that his orders were to take his men to Merano and from there into Germany to fight against the Allies. He emphasised: 'We have no intention of fighting the Italians.'

The Count bluffed, replying: 'I have orders to halt all armed enemy columns and to let no one through. Therefore, I ask you to surrender and I guarantee your safe conduct and that of your men.'

Fallmeyer protested: 'Our High Commands have come to an agreement. We Germans are not to attack the partisans and they are to let us go free.'

'We have no such orders,' the Count replied.

The German said that since leaving Milan everyone had let them through without a shot being fired, which proved there was an agreement.

The Count replied: 'This simply means that you have not come across any partisans, or that those who you did meet were not strong enough to attack you. Here the situation is different. We are in control of the whole area, we are well placed, and I have strong forces at my disposal. You are covered by my mortars and machine guns. I could wipe you all out in 15 minutes.'

The Count and Moretti kept on urging the Lieutenant to surrender, explaining they wanted to avoid bloodshed and that in face of their superior strength it would be disastrous to try and fight it out. But just as strongly he insisted that he would not surrender, that he had to obey orders, and that he did not understand why they were being so obstinate.

As the discussion was proceeding, Lazzaro arrived from Dongo and casually made his way along the column. He counted twenty-eight lorries full of German soldiers, the armoured car, the commanding officer's vehicle, and people in ten cars. In each lorry there was a heavy machine gun, several mortars, and submachine guns. There were also a considerable number of light anti-aircraft guns in the convoy and the men were all in battle order. The Count reflected that the force could have destroyed them and the area they occupied in next to no time at all.

He related: 'Our only hope of salvation lay in mining the Vallorba Bridge. If the Germans were really determined to press on, we would have blown the bridge and trapped them between the mountains on the left and the lake on the right. But there were two problems: to gain the necessary time and find enough explosive. Above all, to gain time. There was nothing for it but a little stratagem.'

The Count told Fallmeyer: 'We have decided that we cannot take the responsibility of allowing you through without orders from our higher command. Our headquarters is a few kilometres away and we will go there for instructions. It would be advisable for one of you to go with us and establish direct contact with them.'

The German seemed unwilling to agree; he was impatient and wanted them to make up their minds there and then.

The Count said: 'I cannot allow you through. If my superior officer gives me the order to do so, I will obey. Otherwise, nothing doing.'

After consulting with other officers, Fallmeyer at last agreed to the Count's proposal and said that he would accompany him to the headquarters with his own vehicle and driver and accompanied by another officer. The Count ordered Lazzaro to return to Dongo to proceed with the mining of the bridge - a single arch construction - and to send a dispatch rider to warn all their roadblocks to let them through, putting as many armed men and unarmed civilians wearing red scarves along the route as possible.

The car carrying the two German officers pulled up and the Count, Moretti, and Hofmann got on board. With rising alarm Fallmeyer took note as they passed through ten well-manned roadblocks and saw large numbers of men in red moving over the lower slopes of hills or in the villages. To add to the effect, the Count warned the driver to slow down every time they came to a bridge, saying that it was mined.

The car finally reached Ponte del Passo, at the northern tip of the lake, where the partisans had twenty men. They stopped at the end of the bridge and were met by Guglielmo Cantoni (Sandrino), another of the main characters in our story, described by the Count as 'one of the bravest and best of the Puecher men,' who was in command. Getting out of the vehicle, the Count asked: 'All men in position here? Mines ready?'

As he saw his commander wink, Cantoni replied: 'Yes, everything ready. Let me know when I have to light the fuses.'

The Count asked him for news of Dionisio Gambaruto (Nicola), commanding officer of the First Lombardy Division, to which the 52nd Brigade belonged. It seemed that he was in Chiavenna, where fighting was going on between partisans and a strong force of Germans and Fascists who were unwilling to surrender.

The Count quickly decided that it was too dangerous to take the Germans that far, as if they knew that a couple of hundred of their men were still holding out, they might try to join them. So he decided to leave the enemy trio in the company of another group of their countrymen who had surrendered the barracks in the neighbouring village of Nuova Olonio on the previous day.

The Count told Fallmeyer that they were going ahead in their own transport, as though their commander was only a kilometre or two away, they had not been able to warn the roadblocks that they were coming and might be fired on. The Lieutenant agreed and the Count left him, his aide, the driver, and Hofmann and commandeered a car on the spot and drove to Chiavenna with Moretti.

They found Gambaruto on the square in front of the station just as the first shooting began; they had not met before, but knew each other by reputation. After hasty introductions, the Count explained the situation as briefly as possible. But his commander was too worried about what was going to happen in the town to think about anything else. He told him: 'You know how many men you have, you know your area better than I do. You decide: I leave you a free hand. All I ask is that you don't bring them here.'

They shook hands and parted after wishing one another well. On the way back, the Count discussed the next move with Moretti.

Since the morning their defences had been strengthened and by now explosive might have been found for mining the Vallorba Bridge. They decided to also mine the Ponte del Passo and, if the worse came to the worse, stop the Germans there.

This only left the problem of the Fascists. They would be more likely to fight and if they decided to do so the Germans would probably join in as well. So the pair decided that they would have to split the two parties, leaving deciding on how this could be done until later.

They collected Hofmann and the Germans from Nuova Olonio and set off on the return journey. The Count told Fallmeyer that they would inform him of their decisions once they were back in Dongo. The party arrived there just after one in the afternoon and Lazzaro told the Count that he had finally succeeded in mining the Vallorba Bridge after obtaining enough explosive. Now the column would no longer be able to pass without a hard fight.

The Count looked the German Lieutenant in the eye and told him firmly: 'Firstly, permission to proceed is granted only to German vehicles and German soldiers; all Italians and all civilian vehicles must therefore be handed over to us. Secondly, all German vehicles must halt at Dongo to be searched and all German personnel must produce identity documents. Thirdly, you will stop again at Ponte del Passo to await further authorisation to proceed.'

At first, Fallmeyer said that he could not betray the trust the Italians had put in him, nor could he fail to protect them or abandon them in their hour of need. The Count refused to give in and decided to give him half an hour to discuss the matter with his men.

Meanwhile, a partisan came from the direction of Musso and said that there were important Fascists in the car at the end of the convoy who were trying to escape to Como. The Count immediately sent ten men along the length of the column with orders to stop anyone getting away. The priest of Musso, Don Enea Mainetti, recalled that when he was about to go into his house just after midday one of the fugitives approached him and said that he wanted to give himself up to a partisan. As he went through the gate he told the priest that Mussolini was in the column as well.

Don Mainetti called one of the partisans and the Fascist was able to surrender to him. Then another civilian appeared and said: 'I am Romano, a government minister. I have my little son with me. I am leaving him in your care because I do not know what will become of me.' Don Mainetti agreed and sent them into his house. Immediately afterwards more civilians called on him, saying that they were well-known people and asking him to speak up for them.

Don Mainetti became the negotiator between the Fascists and the partisans and arranged the peaceful surrender of most of the men. The Count then appeared on the scene, together with Captain Davide Barbiere of the *Alpini* mountain troops, who had assumed command of the volunteers in Musso. The priest told the Count: 'Mussolini's here. Search everywhere, look in every corner. Don't let him get away, because we're sure he's here.'

The Count said later that he did not actually recall who told him that Mussolini was in the column, probably because it did not register much at the time, as there were so many wild rumours flying around. As a result, he was only following routine when he ordered Lazzaro to check the German lorries once they arrived in Dongo, after telling him what he had heard about the dictator. Lazzaro did not take the rumour very seriously either.

Fallmeyer came back after 40 minutes and said: 'Your conditions are accepted. However, you must confirm this with the occupants of the armoured car.'

The Count agreed and with Moretti and Lazzaro walked up to a group of men who were sitting on a low wall and talking by the vehicle. One of them stepped forward and said that he was in command. He was older than the rest, had been wounded in the

Abyssinian war, and wore a Gold Medal for Military Valour pinned to his lapel. He introduced himself as Colonel Francesco Barracu, Under-Secretary to the Presidency of the Council, and said that two of his companions were also senior officers: Vito Casalinuovo and Idreno Utimpergher. When asked what his intentions were, Barracu replied: 'To continue with the German column, naturally. The question seems quite unnecessary.' The partisans thought he could be playing for time, hoping for reinforcements from Como or Menaggio, which would enable them to force the blockade.

The Count told him that an agreement had been concluded under which the column would be splitting up. The Germans did not want to fight any more and as a result his party would be left on their own. Barracu still insisted that he wanted to move on. When pressed for a reason, he said that he had sworn that he would make for Trieste to help defend the city against the Slavs.

As the argument continued, the Count decided that it was now the moment to try to divide the enemy forces. Without much hope of success, he said to Barracu: 'You can see that the Germans are getting agitated. As we have still not reached an agreement, I think that it might be better to let them proceed at least as far as Dongo, then we can continue our discussions in peace.' To the Count's surprise, Barracu agreed almost at once.

The Count went back to the German commander and told him that he could give the order for his column to move off, reminding him that they would have to stop in Dongo for an inspection to be carried out. Fallmeyer replied that the armoured car had to be moved first, as it was in the middle of the road and blocking the way for the lorries. The Count returned to Barracu and he gave the necessary order. The vehicle lumbered to the side of the road and left the way free. The Lieutenant gave his orders to his men, saluted the Count, and happily left for Dongo at the head of the column.

As the lorries drove by the soldiers leaned out, waving their hands and shouting cheerful farewells. The three Fascists with the Count cursed them loudly as they passed. After further discussions, Barracu asked to be allowed to return to Como to report to Marshal Graziani.

The Fascist's obstinacy made the Count suddenly remember that he had been told that there was the possibility that Mussolini was in the convoy, and he asked to search the armoured car. Barracu did not seem at all worried and the Count went into the vehicle through the back door to carry out an inspection. He made his way over the legs of about ten men who were sitting there armed to the teeth and looking at him grimly. The Count inspected their faces one by one until he got to the driver's seat and then turned back; he didn't recognise any of them.

After consulting Moretti the Count told Barracu: 'We have decided to agree to your request. I warn you, however, that if you try to move forward we will open fire.' He looked at his watch. It was seven minutes to three. 'At 3.15 p.m. you may move off,' he concluded. The Count went back to Barracu for the last time and they saluted and shook hands. Then the commander set off for Musso together with Moretti.

Captain Barbieri saw them as they entered the village and called them into his house. The Count was raising a glass of milk to his lips when he heard a burst of machine gun fire, followed by the sound of mortars, rifles, and grenades. He ran with the others to the window, but the street was deserted. They climbed onto the mountainside overlooking the village to see where the noise was coming from and eventually came upon a group of partisans and learned that the armoured car had moved off in a forward direction, firing as it went. Their men had replied and had stopped the vehicle with hand grenades, whereupon most of the occupants began to surrender.

Two of the Fascists had tried to escape by hiding among the rocks close to the water. A boat with several partisans on board arrived from Dongo to search for them. Paolo Porta surrendered immediately, while Alessandro Pavolini was hit by gunfire and was captured later.

Mussolini's natural daughter, Elena Curti Cucciati, remained in the armoured car and began tearing up as many documents as she could, but when she finally looked out to see what was going on discovered that everyone else had gone. She decided to jump out of the back of the vehicle and to make a run for it, but as soon as she picked herself up from the ground a partisan shouted at her to put her hands up. Elena finally managed to persuade him and his companions that she had only hitched a lift in the armoured car, and had nothing to do with the troops inside, and to her surprise was taken into Dongo and told that she was free to go.

The Count was staggered that Barracu had gone back on his word, but before he could think about that for very long he was called away to inspect prisoners from the convoy who had been assembled in a nearby building. He reassured them, had the room cleared of inquisitive onlookers, and ordered that a nominal list of the captives be compiled.

The Count prepared to return to Dongo and on the way he saw Lazzaro and another partisan coming towards him. He recalled: 'Bill said, just as if it were an ordinary piece of news: "I have captured Mussolini in Dongo. I arrested him myself. He is under strict guard and in the town hall." I received the news rather coldly, perhaps not quite realising its importance. It just seemed like an additional load of trouble.'

'All right, let's go and see,' the Count replied. They set off for Dongo and on the way Lazzaro told him what had happened.

7 THE CAPTURE OF MUSSOLINI

The vanguard of the large German convoy packed the town square in Dongo, which was flanked on three sides by neo-classical buildings, with Lake Como at the open end and the snow-covered Alps as a background. The troops were eager to be on their way, but their stay was to last for almost nine hours.

On his return to Dongo, Fallmeyer gave Birzer a brief summary of the agreement he had concluded with the partisans. The SS man agreed that there was no alternative, but said that as no Italian would be able to pass, he was going to put Mussolini in one of the trucks, adding: 'It's our only chance. My orders are to prevent him falling into the wrong hands. If we leave him here...'

Fallmeyer replied: 'Do what you think best, it's your problem.'

Birzer ordered one of the *Luftwaffe* sergeants to give Mussolini his coat and steel helmet to wear. Captain Kisnat of the secret security service was present, but did not say anything. On the other hand, Claretta Petacci begged Mussolini to listen to the Lieutenant's advice. So, even though rather unwillingly, he put the coat on, placed the helmet under his arm, and climbed onto a German lorry, from the rear seat so as not to be seen by the partisans who were in front of the column. Birzer walked around to carry out a final inspection, but caught sight of Mussolini's scared eyes staring out from the spaces between the planks that formed the sides of the truck. 'Hide, *Duce*,' he said, 'don't look out.' They were the last words he ever spoke to him.

Lazzaro was examining the documents of the German soldiers in the second lorry, and not thinking at all of the warning that Mussolini might be in the convoy, when he heard someone shouting his name in great excitement. It was Giuseppe Negri, known as Zocolin, a local clog-maker who had previously been in gaol for three months for helping the partisans.

'Bill, we've got the big bastard,' he said.
'You're dreaming.'
'No, no, Bill, it is Mussolini, I've seen him with my own eyes.'
'You can't have. You must have made a mistake.'
'I swear it, Bill, it is him.'
'Where did you see him?'
'Here on a lorry, dressed as a German.'

Negri told Lazzaro that he had climbed onto the vehicle to check the Germans' documents. Standing nearby was Chief Marshal of the Finance Guards, Francesco Di Paola, who told him to carry out the search meticulously, as the attitude of the soldiers on board was suspicious. Another Finance Guard, with the same rank, Francesco Nanci, who had left his command in Rho, near Milan, to help the partisans, warned Fallmeyer against ordering any violent action and covered the Germans on the lorry with his machine gun. [1]

Negri inspected the documents one by one and there was still more to come from a man huddled up by the driver's cab with his back against the left hand side of the vehicle.

The partisan could not see his face, because he had raised the collar of his greatcoat and pulled his helmet down. Negri went to ask for his papers, but the Germans in the lorry stopped him and said: 'Comrade drunk, Comrade drunk,' and made gestures of someone lifting a drink to their lips.

Negri took no notice and went up to the figure. There was a pile of blankets near him and one of them covered his shoulders. The partisan sat down beside him and pulled his greatcoat collar down. He never moved.

Negri continued with his story: 'I only saw him side-face, but I recognised him at once, Bill. It is Mussolini, I swear it. I recognised him. As the Germans were armed, I didn't let on I knew and got down. Di Paola asked me what was wrong, but I didn't reply and came to find you.'

Negri led Lazzaro to the fourth lorry in the convoy. He looked inside and saw the shape huddled up against the driver's seat with his back to him. As the clog-maker had said, he was wearing a German helmet and a greatcoat with the collar turned up.

Lazzaro tapped the man on the shoulder and said: 'Comrade.' He didn't move or reply.

'Your Excellency,' Lazzaro cried, still tapping him on the shoulder. There was again no word or gesture in response.

Finally, Lazzaro yelled: '*Cavalier* Benito Mussolini.' The form gave a start. By now a small crowd had gathered around the lorry and the Germans were looking jumpy.

Lazzaro grabbed hold of the side of the vehicle and jumped on board. The man remained silent and motionless. His helmet was pulled down over his eyes and his coat collar entirely covered his face. Lazzaro recalled: 'I took his helmet off and saw his bald pate and the shape of his head. I took his sunglasses off and turned the collar of his greatcoat down. It was him, Mussolini!'

He was holding a machine gun between his knees, with the butt underneath his chin. Lazzaro took it from him and handed it to his driver, a man called Battista Pirali. Lazzaro helped Mussolini to get up and asked him 'Have you got any other weapons' He did not answer, but unbuttoned his greatcoat and pulled out a long-barrelled Glisenti automatic revolver from his waistband, which the partisan stuffed into his pocket.

Questioned after the war as to why his men had not used force to prevent Mussolini from being captured, Birzer said that his orders had been to escort and guard him, to prevent him at all costs from escaping if he attempted to do so, and to defend him in case of necessity. But the situation at Musso and Dongo did not allow him to use force.

Lieutenant Fallmeyer, who was commandant of the column, had signed precise agreements with the partisan commanders of the zone according to which only German soldiers had freedom of transit. Therefore, he could neither resist nor give orders to the two hundred men who answered to Fallmeyer.

Birzer stated that the experience at Dongo was the worst of his life. However, he thought that he acted wisely and according to conscience. For the rest, no one could have imagined that Mussolini would be recognised wearing German military uniform and sunglasses.

Birzer concluded: 'What should I have done? Decide on useless bloodshed? Continue, with thirty or forty men, a war that was practically over in Italy? I have nothing to reproach myself with. I was not a General; I was a simple Second-Lieutenant, a simple soldier.'

A large crowd of townspeople had gathered around the lorry and they were beginning to shout. The Germans handed over their weapons to appease them, evidently fearing reprisals after trying to conceal Mussolini despite their agreement with the partisans.

'In the name of the Italian people, I arrest you,' said Lazzaro to Mussolini, and the noise from the crowd rose to a crescendo.

'I will not do anything,' the dictator replied dreamily, as if to say: 'I will not resist.'

Lazzaro told him: 'I give my word that so long as you remain in my personal charge, no one will touch a hair of your head,' realising it was rather a silly thing to say to an almost completely bald man.

'Thank you,' he replied.

Lazzaro and Pirali went to help Mussolini down, all the time fearing that the Germans would open fire, but on the contrary they lowered the tailboard of the lorry for them.

The dictator is said to have muttered 'Will no one here defend me?' The two partisans pushed their way through the braying crowd and led him 60 metres or so towards the town hall in the square, the Palazzo Manzi, which had once accommodated Napoleon.

The townspeople began to scream: 'They've got Mussolini,' and some bawled out insults as well. He turned around to look at them, his brow puckering with fear. The newly installed Mayor of Dongo, Doctor Giuseppe Rubini, told him: 'Don't worry. No harm will come to you here.'

'I'm sure of that. The people of Dongo are generous,' Mussolini replied, remembering a previous visit.

They crossed the threshold of the town hall and Lazzaro asked him: 'Where is your son Vittorio?'

'I don't know,' he replied, lowering his head.

'And Marshal Graziani?'

'I don't know. I think he is in Como,' he replied, this time looking at Lazzaro.

Mussolini was taken to a long, simply furnished room with two windows overlooking the square. He sat down on a bench against a wall and removed his German greatcoat. He was wearing a black shirt, a pair of militia officers' cavalry trousers, and riding boots, but no jacket.

Lazzaro asked him: 'Why ever were you on the lorry with the Germans, when your ministers were in the armoured car?'

'I don't know, they put me there. Perhaps they betrayed me in the end.'

'What?'

'They put me in there.'

Lazzaro placed four partisans in the room, telling their officer in a voice loud enough for Mussolini to hear: 'No one must disturb the prisoner. See that he is taken care of and use your gun if necessary.' Four guards were also posted outside the door with orders not to let anyone in without permission.

As Lazzaro was about to return to the column the door suddenly burst open and four more prisoners were escorted in by two partisans. 'Hail *Duce*,' said Barracu, Casalinuovo, Utimpergher, and

Porta, standing stiffly to attention. He gave them a lazy nod of his head.

In the absence of the doctor, Lazzaro called for the pharmacist to be brought to see to Barracu's wound and ordered the clearing of onlookers from the premises. Then he resumed his inspection of the convoy.

A partisan again attracted his attention, this time with the strange story of a Spanish Consul in the column. He reported that the man's documents seemed to be in order and that he wanted to leave urgently for Switzerland. Lazzaro decided to see for himself. The partisan took him to a low Alfa-Romeo, yellow in colour, which had been driven to the head of the column. At the wheel was a fair-haired, stocky man with a small birthmark on his chin. A young woman sat alongside him, and their two young boys were in the back with another lady whose face was partially hidden in the collar of an expensive fur coat and a turban-shaped hat. The car was piled high with suitcases.

Lazzaro rested his foot on the running board of the vehicle and asked: 'Are you the Spanish Consul?'

The man turned to him and snapped: 'Yes, and I am in a hurry,' in perfect Italian.

'May I see your papers, please?'

'I've already shown them to a hundred people.'

'Well, you can show them to me as well.'

The suspect snorted and took three yellow-backed passports out of his pocket, which were printed with 'Spanish Consulate of Milan' and embossed with the country's coat of arms. One of the passports was made out to Juan Muñez y Castillo, another to his wife, and the third to both of them. Lazzaro inspected the documents and saw that they had been fabricated in a hurry. On the joint passport the birth date of the wife was 1912, whereas on the single ones both dates were 1914; in addition, the stamps validating the photographs were inked not printed. 'These passports are fake and you are under arrest,' said Lazzaro.

The lady in front of the car turned pale and the one in the back looked at him imploringly.

The man burst out indignantly: 'What do you mean? You'll pay for this. I have an appointment in Switzerland at seven this evening with a senior Allied official. I am expected. Have you ever seen such impudence?'

'You have fake passports. Follow me,' Lazzaro insisted. 'Drive the car up to the door,' he said, pointing to the town hall, 'and keep quiet, because I'm in charge here.' The three adults and two children were taken inside and their suitcases were unloaded from the car.

The inspection of the convoy had lasted between 30 and 45 minutes and it must have been more or less four in the afternoon when Mussolini was unexpectedly found and captured.

8 THE GERMAN SURRENDER

When the Count and Moretti got back to Dongo after hearing Lazzaro's account of the capture of Mussolini, they found a large crowd in the square outside the town hall making threats and hurling abuse at the prisoners inside. However, they were well protected by the four guards in the room and the other four outside the doors.

As soon as the Count went into the room he saw Mussolini sitting at a large table by the door. He looked bewildered and fearful. The Count assured him that he was safe, and he thanked him and said that everyone was behaving correctly.

The Count also saw Barracu, who was having his right arm bandaged after a slight shrapnel wound. When asked why the armoured car had tried to move forward and began firing, he replied that they started to turn the vehicle around and the partisans opened fire; naturally, they had replied.

Lazzaro informed the Count that the Spaniard he told him about was in a small room on the left of the hall. The commander found the man with a tall, fair-haired woman, whom he said was his wife, two blonde young boys, another woman, and an air force officer.

The suspect said that he was a diplomat attached to the embassy in Milan on an important mission to meet a senior Allied official in Switzerland that evening. The Count replied that his documents were not in order and that in any event the roads were too dangerous to travel. So for now he would not be allowed to proceed.

At that moment the younger of the two children ran to his mother and, pulling her by the hand, said: 'Mummy, why are we waiting here? Why can't we go? Is it these stupid partisans who won't let us go?'

The airman introduced himself as Captain Pietro Calistri of the Republican Air Force and said that he had joined the column by pure chance; unfortunately he was mistaken for Mussolini's pilot.

The Count turned to the unknown lady sitting down, whom he described as pretty and extremely tired - who was in fact Claretta Petacci.

He said: 'And who are you, madam?'

'Oh, nobody in particular. I happened to be in Como during the disturbances and to avoid being caught in any danger I asked these people for a lift so that I could get away to somewhere quiet. I've certainly landed myself in a mess now. What are you going to do with me?'

'We'll see to you later,' he replied, and left the room.

Meanwhile, Lazzaro was sitting by Mussolini and drawing up an inventory of the contents of the bags and briefcases of his followers. When he had finished, he turned to a large portfolio in brownish-yellow leather belonging to the dictator himself.

He placed it on the table and was about to open it when Mussolini tugged his arm and said: 'Look, those documents inside are secret. I warn you that they are of great historical importance.'

His personal files had been brought to the Villa Feltrinelli from Rome when he was installed as the head of the Italian Social Republic in September 1943. Prior to leaving Lake Garda on 18 April 1945 the documents had been sifted again by his private secretary Luigi Gatti to ensure that only the most important items were brought with them, while the rest were sent on ahead to Como, but, as we have seen, soon fell into the hands of the partisans.

Lazzaro hesitated for a moment and then opened the portfolio. It had three divisions and inside each one there was a bundle of folders tied with blue ribbon and marked 'Secret, for the attention of Benito Mussolini.' The first files covered both the possibility of escape into Switzerland and the political situation in Trieste; the second, consisted of correspondence between Mussolini and Hitler; and the third dealt with the Verona trial of 1944 of some of those who had helped overthrow the dictator the year before.

At the bottom of the portfolio, Lazzaro also found one hundred and sixty-three gold sovereigns, which Mussolini said were intended for his most trusted friends, and seven cheques issued by Italian banks for amounts between twenty-five thousand Lire and half a million Lire. Lazzaro subsequently deposited the documents and the money in the savings bank at Domaso.

Another bag was confiscated from Mussolini's Liaison Officer, Colonel Vito Casalinuovo, which contained the wallets of Barracu and Pavolini; some documents belonging to Federal Commissar of Como, Paolo Porta; cheques to the value of 1,700,000 Lire; and 160 Pounds Sterling.

The Count and Lazzaro recovered the two bags from the bank on 2 May and for greater security entrusted them to the parish priest of Gera Lario, Don Franco Gusmaroli, who hid them behind the alter of his church. It remained to be decided who would be given the documents, since they could not remain hidden for very long. The partisans decided to consult General Cadorna in Milan and in an interview with Brigadier Antonio Scappin of the Finance Guards he advised that they should be brought to the central Military Committee until the National Liberation Committee decided what should be done with them.

The files were inspected in the priest's house by the Count and Lazzaro and then picked up by Scappin to take to Palazzo Brera in Milan. However, at the last moment, Michele Moretti, Political Commissar of the 52nd Brigade, intervened to ensure that the documents were first seen by the local military committee in Como. Its commander, Oreste Gementi (Riccardo), gave a receipt to the Brigadier for 'two parcels sealed by the Savings Bank of Domaso containing the documents seized from Benito Mussolini at the time of his arrest in Dongo.' However, the members of the committee were disappointed at the contents, Gementi relating that they discovered 'no document of any importance.' The files were finally delivered to General Cadorna on 16 May, who in turn handed them over to the Minister of War of the Italian Government, Alessandro Casati, on 21 June.

Far from the documents contained in Mussolini's famous bag disappearing, as claimed by some theorists, they then made their way to Allied Force Headquarters, together with other captured documents, where they were translated, copied, and microfilmed by the Joint Allied Intelligence Agency. In 1947 the files were returned to the Italian Government, with a set of copies being sent to the United States and the United Kingdom, where they are now held by the national archives. They contain no 'secret Churchill-Mussolini correspondence.'

Back in the town hall in Dongo on 27 April, the Count ordered two partisans to escort the pseudo-Spaniard, his wife, and their two children to the hotel. As the commander was looking over the man's documents brought to him by Lazzaro he heard loud shouting in the square. A boat at the jetty was bringing the prisoners ashore who had run towards the lake when the other occupants of the armoured car surrendered.

Paolo Porta had been recaptured almost immediately and Alessandro Pavolini had hidden among the rocks. The crowd recognised him and were closing on him menacingly, until the Count got him away. He was provided with dry clothing, and a slight chest wound was attended to by the local pharmacist in the absence of the doctor.

The Count ordered Scappin, who was commander of the Finance Guards at Gera Lario, to return to the upper lake to obtain the disarmament of the German convoy when it made its agreed halt at Ponte del Passo. Brigadier Giorgio Buffelli accompanied the German commander in his car at the head of the column, which displayed a white flag as a sign of surrender together with the red flag of the partisans. Scappin arrived at the bridge on a motorcycle and gave the necessary orders. He told the German that he would not allow them to continue and demanded their unconditional surrender; otherwise he would obliterate them with the canons of the fort of Colico, which had just been occupied by the partisans.

Fallmeyer took the bait and immediately asked to see a senior partisan commander. He was sent to the new headquarters in Morbegno, with Hofmann as interpreter, and it was agreed that the unconditional surrender would come into effect at nine in the morning.

However, when the party returned to Gera, Scappin was angry at the outcome. He recalled: 'I thought it imprudent to leave them for the whole night, united and armed; aware of the danger they represented I told the German officer that I could not grant him any further delay, that he had to surrender immediately, and that if he did not I would put in place the attack plan that I had already prepared.' Fallmeyer finally agreed.

With Lazzaro, who had arrived from Dongo, Scappin and Hofmann took the German lieutenant and one of his officers in their car to draft the surrender document in Morbegno. A dispatch rider went ahead to warn all the roadblocks to let them through. The party found the area commander, known as Maio, at his headquarters in the elementary school and after an hour an agreement was drawn up. The Germans were to hand over all weapons and war material, but could keep any other personal possessions and would be allowed to cross into Switzerland or to travel in any other direction they chose.

The party went back along the road to Ponte del Passo, accompanied by a rebel commander known as Andrea, who took over responsibility for overseeing the final transit of the convoy. The German commander gave his men the news of the surrender and many of them came to shake the hands of the partisans.

When he returned to his base at Gera Lario, Scappin was advised that the military committee in Milan had asked to speak to him urgently on the telephone, using the private line of the Como Hydro-Electric Society. The Brigadier informed his leaders that Mussolini had been captured. Two hours later he was called again and received the order 'to guard Mussolini, without hurting him, and to treat him well,' with the additional instruction: 'rather than hurt him, let him go.' Scappin replied that they would guard him well without mistreating him and that the order would be passed on immediately to the Count in Dongo, which was carried out by a courier.

Lazzaro and Scappin set off again for Domaso and on the way crossed paths with two German naval officers in a Fiat who said they had just surrendered to the partisans at Dongo. They were put in temporary accommodation at the Albergo Italia in Gravedona, but were then found to be in possession of thirty-three million Lire in one thousand denomination banknotes.

They offered Hofmann eleven million Lire if he divided the rest evenly between two of their lady friends. He pretended to agree, so as to take possession of the money, which he hid in his cellar. With Lazzaro he decided that they would take the banknotes to a safe place, so that that they could eventually be handed over to the Italian Government. In the meantime, they decided on secrecy, both to avoid possible theft by armed gangs and to keep the money out of the hands of the Allied High Command.

The Germans camped out overnight and got rid of everything that might compromise them in the final search of their vehicles in the morning. Many documents had been given to them by the Fascist leaders when they separated and Birzer and Fallmeyer decided that the items should now be burnt, together with any paper money.

The Germans were finally disarmed and ordered to abandon their vehicles. Two heavy suitcases of crocodile skin, or similar material, which were loaded with gold, diamonds, and other precious objects, were each lifted by four men and thrown into the River Mera, one breaking open on impact.

The next morning, a fisherman crossing the river by boat saw something glittering on the river bed. He began dredging the waters as best he could and eventually ended up with scraps and pieces of gold totalling thirty-six kilos in weight. He handed these over to the Count in a sack on the same evening, who tipped the contents out on Hofmann's table.

They were amazed to discover that the heap of gold was composed of thousands of rings and other items contributed by the public to the war effort at the time of the Abyssinian campaign ten years earlier and still unused. The Count recalled: 'I therefore took care to keep that gold well hidden, as well as the millions of Lire, until the time came to hand it all over to our government.'

The partisans finally took the Germans on foot over the mountains to the border with Switzerland and they were then allowed to walk in the countryside towards Germany. It was while making his way through a little Swiss village that Mussolini's onetime bodyguard, Fritz Birzer, first heard the news that he had been executed.

In June 1945, a month after the end of the war in Europe, Birzer, was arrested by the Americans and spent three years in eleven different prison camps. During this period he was interrogated at length by agents of the OSS and then by those of its successor organisation, the Central Intelligence Agency.

9 MOVING MUSSOLINI

After the initial excitement surrounding the capture of Mussolini, Count Pier Luigi Bellini delle Stelle and his closest collaborators had to decide what to do next.

The orders from their leaders in Milan were that they should take all possible precautions to prevent his escape or liberation. But the local partisans felt that holding him in the town hall in Dongo was far too dangerous, as it could be easily reached by the enemy, who might fall on them at any moment.

The Count devised a complicated plan that would keep Mussolini's final destination secret by first taking him to a safe place nearby and then moving him to the preferred location later.

For the initial transfer, the Count asked for the advice of Brigadier Giorgio Buffelli of the Dongo Finance Guards and he suggested taking Mussolini to the barracks at Germasino, as it lent itself to defence. The Count agreed at once.

The small village is located in the mountains overlooking the lake at almost six hundred metres above sea level, but is less than five kilometres from Dongo. The detachment was responsible for monitoring the nearby border with Switzerland and its men had often lent weapons to the partisans, provided shelter during cold winter nights, and even supplied occasional recruits.

For the second move, the Count consulted Luigi Canali, who was very familiar with the lake area. He said that he knew the ideal spot 'on the outskirts of Como in the house of trusted friends.' This was an Alpine hut at San Maurizio, above Como, where he had taken shelter in June 1944 and was about an hour's car journey away.

After taking these decisions the Count sent a small patrol to keep watch on Germasino and arranged for a car to pick him and Buffelli up outside the town hall in Dongo at 6.30 p.m. For secrecy a column of ten partisans was lined up between the entrance and the car so that no one could see as Mussolini was being led out. As there was a spare place in the vehicle the Count decided to take Commissar Paolo Porta as well. They quickly got into the car. The Count sat next to the driver and Buffelli was in the back between Mussolini on the left and Porta on the right. They set off up the narrow, winding road, followed by the escort of young partisans in a lorry.

During the journey, Mussolini asked several times where they were and where they were going. Buffelli answered vaguely: 'We are in the mountains of the Dongo Valley.' Mussolini seemed rather nervous and restless, especially as he noticed that the Brigadier kept his gun in his hand with the safety catch removed and ready to fire.

The Count turned and offered the dictator a cigarette, but he refused, saying that he rarely smoked and then only the lightest tobacco. He was questioned about the torture suffered by partisans who fell into the hands of the Fascists and was vigorously denying any responsibility when at about 7 p.m. they arrived at the barracks in Germasino, a commandeered three-story villa, which after the war would revert to domestic use.

They were welcomed by Brigadier Antonio Spadea, commander of the detachment, and by Chief Marshal Francesco Nanci, the former commander, who had made his own way there after helping check the convoy in Dongo during the afternoon. Mussolini and Porta were led into the barracks and taken to Spadea's office. After a while they made it clear that they were cold. Porta accepted a blanket, which he put on like a shawl, while Mussolini preferred to walk around the room to warm up.

A stark but airy cell on the first floor was cleared of storage items and a camp bed and mattress were brought in for him; Porta was put in the barracks room and arrangements were made for some of the other prisoners from Dongo to be brought there in the morning.

At around 7.20 p.m. the Count placed Buffelli on guard duty, as he was about to leave. He told him that Mussolini was to be treated with every consideration and that his wishes should be respected whenever possible, as long as they did not conflict with his safe custody.

The Count asked the dictator if he wanted anything. He replied that he had no personal needs but begged him to tell the lady that was travelling with the Spanish Consul that he was well, that he sent her his regards, and that she was not to worry about him.

Taken aback, the Count replied: 'Certainly, if that is all, but tell me, who is the lady?'

'Well, you see, she is a close friend...'

'You could at least tell me her name if I am expected to speak to her.'

Mussolini reluctantly whispered: 'It is *Signora* Petacci,' and gazed at the Count to see his reaction.

However, the revelation did not make a great impression on him. He knew vaguely that she had been his mistress for several years, but there was nothing very extraordinary in that, and besides, she had not attracted much attention.

So, he merely replied: 'All right, 'I'll give her your message.'

The Count left the barracks after warning his men to keep a close watch on the prisoners. On the way back to Dongo it occurred to him that what was happening was almost beyond belief. Mussolini, Petacci, and most of the ministers of the Fascist Government were all in his hands and almost without a struggle. Where were all those faithful followers who had sworn to defend him to the last bullet?

Back at Germasino, Brigadier Buffelli remained alone in the office with Mussolini for some time. Though downcast and tired, he wanted to talk, and began by asking where he was. The Brigadier confirmed that they were in the barracks of the Finance Guards. He recalled that their subsequent conversation was very fragmentary and incomplete because Mussolini changed the subject if he did not like the topic.

At about nine o'clock, Brigadier Spadea personally served the evening meal to the two prisoners. Mussolini dined on risotto, roast kid, and vegetable omelette, and afterwards asked for some tea, which he drank with evident relish. After the meal, Spadea and the other officers tried to engage him in conversation, and though he refused to discuss recent events in Italy he responded readily to questions on international relations.

Afterwards, he walked up and down to warm his feet and to ease his digestion, or so he told Buffelli. While he was strolling, he turned to him and said: 'You played a fine card by stopping us, as the Germans had orders to use force immediately.'

'We were completely determined,' the Brigadier replied, 'because the present situation was unbearable and could not continue. Anyway, now it's done and it's gone well; let's just hope that there's no rescue attempt, since either we all go out together or nobody goes out.'

Mussolini stopped, looked at him and, almost taking on a friendly air, said: 'No, it's not possible, those were other times.'

Finally, holding a pen and half a sheet of foolscap paper, Buffelli asked: 'Would you mind writing a couple of lines?'

''What is it, an interrogation report?'

'No, only a statement that we captured you.'

'That's fine then, if it's for the historical record.'

He wrote to the Brigadier's dictation: 'The 52nd Garibaldi Brigade captured me today, Friday, 27 April, in the square of Dongo,' and added on his own initiative: 'During and after capture I have been treated correctly. Signed, Mussolini.' Buffelli thanked him and put the paper in his pocket, handing it to the Count later.

All the officers had the opportunity to speak with their prisoner. They began by recounting the misdeeds of the various militias and criticising the way their own service had been treated, but he limited himself to listening and staying silent. Porta intervened and said that the topics were upsetting him and that they should desist. Ignoring this injunction, Chief Marshal Nanci told Mussolini that only criminals supported the Fascist Republic and that no one else believed in him anymore, which finally provoked a reaction from the dictator:

Only a short time ago I made the last of many attempts to persuade Ribbentrop to change course and to listen to different opinions, but he replied that this would have led to the mistrust of German power, which was still intact, and adversely affect the military situation, as well as politics and society. As always I believed in the Germans, but I was deceived and also betrayed many times; I was their prisoner and their slave; they followed me everywhere and set the duration of my meetings. They were cowards, because not only did they prevent me from escaping but let me be captured. All they did was to throw blankets over me until I nearly suffocated. [1]

At 11.30 p.m. the prisoners expressed their desire to go and rest and Buffelli accompanied Mussolini to the cell prepared for him. The Brigadier asked if the covers were sufficient and, after feeling their weight like some tourist, the dictator said that they were fine. Buffelli took an old grey blanket that he happened to find and put it as a bedside rug. Mussolini thanked him warmly.

'So you see that you are not in the hands of common criminals,' the Brigadier said, 'rest assured, and good night.'

'Good night,' he replied.

Back in Dongo, the Count went to see Petacci in a small room on the ground floor of the town hall and they had a conversation lasting for an hour or more. At first she denied knowing Mussolini, but when the commander got up as if to leave she gave a deep sigh and said: 'Yes, it is true, I am Clara Petacci. I trust you and hope that you will not deceive me. Tell me what message did he send me?

Where is he now? Is he in danger? How is he? Who has got him? Who is in command here?'

The Count replied: 'Calm down, madam, please. I am in command here. Mussolini is in my charge and I can tell you that, for the moment at least, he is not in danger.'

The commander passed on the brief message from her lover and she then asked: 'How long will he be in your hands? Who will you hand him over to?' The Count replied that the Milan headquarters had been informed and that he was waiting for instructions. She broke in: 'But you ought to hand him over to the Allies. He would be safer with them.'

The Count gave a revealing response: 'The Allies? But I am an Italian. I am a soldier in the Italian army. I am in my own headquarters and responsible only to my government. The Allies have nothing to do with it. On the contrary I shall do what I can to see that he doesn't fall into their hands.' As a lawyer, he was in favour of bringing Mussolini to trial and punishment, a prospect that appalled Petacci, as she could guess the eventual outcome.

As the Count was about to leave, she asked him to grant her a favour, saying that it was the only thing that would make her happy and take away some of the anguish of her present situation. She began to tell him about her life and her relationship with Mussolini and burst into tears many times, which deeply touched the young commander. Finally, she looked at him with a gleam of hope in her eyes, fell silent for a moment, and then suddenly leaned forward slightly and grasped his hand, saying: 'Let me be with him.'

He was taken aback and hesitated before replying, so that Petacci began to suspect that the partisans intended to shoot Mussolini. She said: 'I want to die with him. My life will mean nothing once he is dead. I would die anyway, but more slowly and with greater suffering. That is all I am asking: to die with him. You can't deny me that.'

The Count gave her his word that he had no intention of shooting Mussolini and said that he had already told her he was going to hand him over to the Italian authorities. As he left, he promised that he would do whatever he could to meet her wish to be reunited with him.

Meanwhile, the local pharmacist, Franco Mancini, had been called in to treat wounded prisoners - Barracu and Pavolini - with the help of a medical student from Milan. Mancini also saw Petacci and recalled that she asked for a glass of brandy, but left it after taking a sip. An hour later, she also requested a coffee, but refused to drink it, saying that it was not good enough. Shortly afterwards, she cleaned the rim of her glass and drank the brandy all down, saying that she hoped it would not make her ill.

Claretta was wearing a dark brown dress, a turban-shaped hat, and a mink coat, and was carrying another white coat. On her right wrist was a gold chain with a little padlock and a military-style identity disc. She was wearing a wedding ring on her left hand and a watch on her wrist. A gold powder compact was in her bag.

When Mancini asked her how she came to be with the convoy she replied that she was with friends, still concealing her identity from him. Suddenly, one of the girls from the town burst into the room and said that Petacci had been arrested in the convoy. When she heard this, Claretta looked worried and asked repeatedly what the people were saying about 'that woman Petacci' and if she was likely to be shot.

The Count saw Canali and Moretti coming into the room and told them: 'The woman in the next room is Claretta Petacci.'

They asked: 'How did you find out?'

'Mussolini told me shortly before I left Germasino, then she confirmed it. He begged and implored me not to tell anyone. I really don't think there would be any point in spreading the news around. We'll keep it to ourselves.'

The Count added that she had asked him to allow her to be reunited with Mussolini and that he had no particular objections to the request. His friends agreed and the Count returned to Petacci.

He said: 'Well, madam, we will agree to what you ask. We have decided to put you with him. Are you happy?'

She looked surprised, her face lit up with joy and gratitude, and she said: 'When will you take me to him? Can we go right away?'

'No, not right away. We have to move Mussolini to a safer place and we'll take you to him there.'

'So we'll travel together?'

'I don't know yet. We shall see. Stay here for a little while longer and don't worry. Try to rest because we will not be leaving for two or three hours.'

The Count left her and went to the Dongo Hotel, as the pseudo-Spaniard had asked to see him. It was 10.30 p.m. when they came face to face and the man offered the commander a cigarette from a gold case as they sat down. He asked what decision he had come to and insisted that he had an important diplomatic mission to carry out and that there would be trouble if he was detained any longer. The Count told him that the group's passports were not in order and that they would be held until their identity was confirmed. He saluted and left to find Canali and Moretti at the town hall.

They decided to move Mussolini as soon as possible and to take two cars. As Canali was well known in the area, he would lead in the first vehicle and identify himself at roadblocks, telling the partisans that the second one contained a seriously wounded fighter who had to be taken to Como hospital as soon as possible. Moretti and another partisan would also travel in the first car to escort Petacci, who would play the part of a Red Cross nurse.

The Count was to accompany Mussolini in the second car. His head would be bandaged so that no one would recognise him, as the partisans feared that if anyone found out who he really was they might all be taken for Fascists carrying out a rescue attempt and shot on the spot.

They were to ask for news of the local situation at every road block and, if there was any uncertainty, simply turn around. Two other partisans would also travel in the second car, one of them a young woman, tall and slim, with blue eyes, dark hair, and a deep hatred of Fascists.

She was Giuseppina Tuissi, known as Gianna, who was born at Abbiategrasso, near Milan, on 23 June 1924. Resident in the Baggio area of the city, she first worked for the local Fratelli Borletti firm, manufacturers of precision instruments, but after taking part in a strike in October 1943 was dismissed with fellow workers. Soon afterwards she found employment at the military hospital in Baggio. Her father, Umberto, brother, Cesare, and fiancé, Gianni Alippi (Galippo), were all members of the Third Milanese GAP (*Gruppi di azione patriottica*), a small action group of partisans which operated in the city.

At the military hospital, Giuseppina issued false certificates to soldiers who did not want to go to the front and provided bogus forms, licences, and passes to GAP members at Borletti, including her fiancé Gianni and brother, Cesare. However, Gianni was arrested in Milan on 28 August 1944, tortured all day, and shot in the evening together with three companions.

As Giuseppina's activities had become known to the authorities, to avoid capture she was sent by the Communist partisan command of Milan as a courier to assist Luigi Canali in his work of coordinating the detachments, where she adopted the battle name of Gianna in memory of her fiancé.

Once the plans for the journey were made, the Count said that he would go and pick up Mussolini from Germasino and return in about an hour's time. Meanwhile, Canali and Moretti were to prepare a permit for the transportation of a wounded partisan with a

Red Cross nurse and another showing that the Count was the commander of the 52nd Garibaldi Brigade.

He went out into the square and met Lazzaro, who told him that the German convoy had finally surrendered. He also reported the contact Brigadier Antonio Scappin had made with the partisan command in Milan on the private telephone of the hydro-electric company and that they now knew that Mussolini and his followers had been captured.

Writing after the war, Bellini delle Stelle described the reply received on the same line some time later as 'a mysterious message from some unidentified higher command,' pointing out that it said that Mussolini was to be treated with every regard, that he was not to be touched, and in case he attempted to escape was not to be pursued lest any harm should come to him.

At 10.30 in the evening, Lieutenant-Colonel Luigi Villani of the Finance Guards followed up Scappin's earlier message to the National Liberation Committee in Milan by reporting that while several ministers and other Fascist leaders were being held in Dongo, Mussolini and Paolo Porta were captives in the barracks at Germasino.

The Count told Lazzaro that Mussolini was about to be moved once again and that one of the ladies with the 'Spanish Consul' had been identified as his lover, Claretta Petacci, who would travel with him.

As for the destination, only Canali knew the place, and it was better that way.

10 TURNING BACK

A little after one in the morning on 28 April, the Count and his driver left Dongo in heavy rain to collect Mussolini from the barracks of the Finance Guards in the upland village of Germasino. Every now and then the pitch black night was lit by a flash of lightening that bathed the surrounding countryside in a sudden and rather sinister glare. Not a living soul was to be seen.

Once they arrived at the barracks, a partisan was sent to wake Brigadier Giorgio Buffelli up and to tell him that the Count wanted to talk to him.

'I've come to pick up Mussolini and take him away,' said the commander.

'He's fine,' the Brigadier replied. 'He enjoyed a good meal and spoke to everybody.'

Buffelli went up to the cell, unlocked the door and put the light on, but Mussolini did not wake up.

The Brigadier shook his bed and, with a start, he looked up and asked: 'What is it?'

'The order to leave has arrived,' Buffelli replied.

'I expected it,' he said.

Mussolini got up and they gave him one of the Finance Guard overcoats to replace the German one he had thrown aside with disdain; they closed the door to let him dress and after about ten minutes he was ready.

They all went into the office and the Count said to him: 'Allow me to bandage your face, we must pass several checkpoints and it's best that they do not recognise you.'

'If it's necessary, I've no objection,' he replied.

The Brigadier took the bandage that the Count was holding, removed Mussolini's cap and covered his head so that only his nose, eyes, and mouth were visible.

The Count sat alongside him in the back of the car and they set off at full speed to Dongo. After a few minutes, Mussolini asked if he had been able to speak to Petacci. He confirmed that he had and that she had been happy to receive the message. He then added: 'The lady asked to be allowed to join you and she begged and prayed so earnestly that we decided to agree.'

Surprised and delighted, Mussolini asked where they were taking him.

'Somewhere near Como where you can be kept in the greatest security and secrecy,' the Count replied. 'I shall then wait for further orders. I still have none concerning you.'

They travelled on down to Dongo in silence and as they got to a bridge leading to the ironworks at the entrance to the town the headlights of their car picked out a black Fiat 1500 that was parked on the right hand side of the road. Moretti got out of it and confirmed that everything was ready.

The Count saw that Petacci was also on the roadside, together with Canali, and got Mussolini out of their car too, so that the couple could meet for a moments before the journey resumed.

They exchanged a few hurried words in the pouring rain:

'Good evening, Your Excellency.'

'Good evening, madam.'

'Why have you followed me?'

'Because I wanted to. But what has happened to you? Are you wounded?'

'No, it's nothing, merely a precaution.'

The Count, Canali, and Moretti agreed on the last arrangements for the journey. If the lead vehicle lost sight of the other, it was to stop and wait, and if this lasted for any length of time they were to turn around and see what had happened.

Canali and Moretti returned to their car and Tuissi got out of it to join the Count. Guglielmo Cantoni (Sandrino) was sitting next to the driver and Mussolini was in the back between Tuissi on his left and the Count on his right. In the first vehicle, Canali sat beside the driver in the front, while Petacci was in the back between Moretti and another partisan, Giuseppe Frangi (Lino).

They took the road for Como, the cars moving off slowly, keeping a distance of about a hundred metres between them. There was little, if any, coordination between the various partisan units that guarded the different sections of the road, so whenever they came to a roadblock Canali would get out, identify himself, and say that the vehicle following him was carrying a wounded man and that it should be allowed through as a matter of urgency.

All was going well until there was a sudden burst of machine gun fire near the Count's car when it was approaching Menaggio. He ordered the driver to pull in as closely as possible under the shelter of the rocks and stood in the middle of the road shouting and waving his arms. He saw some men hurrying down the slope along a footpath and hurled abuse at them for manning a barrier in this way.

Their officer tried to excuse himself by saying that he had sited his men among the rocks as it was raining; since the first car had driven through the roadblock he had been determined to stop the second one. Canali appeared at that point, having turned back to see what had happened. He was recognised, everything was sorted out, and they set off again.

There was another hold up at when they reached Cadenabbia. This time, Canali was not known at a roadblock and as he argued with local partisans some of them began to approach the second car containing Mussolini. Fortunately, the Count saw that one of them was a young man called Angelo, who had been with him in the Puecher detachment and had then joined another unit of the brigade. After exchanging friendly greetings, the Count explained what they were doing and they were allowed to proceed.

Moretti recalled that Canali knew the password required at the roadblocks only as far as Argegno, so that the farther journey southwards was problematic. At Brienno a burst of machine gun fire was directed at the lead car, but it went wide.

When they reached Moltrasio the Count saw the other car stop in the square. Canali jumped out and waved at them to pull in. When the engines were switched off they could hear the sound of gunfire and Canali went to ask a friend for information. The news was vague but disturbing. It seemed that the Allies had reached Como during the evening and were fighting pockets of Fascists in the streets.

Moretti recalled: 'We learned later that the firing arose from celebrations on the arrival of the Allies. Bellini delle Stelle and Canali insisted on making for San Maurizio, avoiding Como. For my part, I opposed this, making them aware of the possibility of an encounter with the Allies and inevitably having to hand Mussolini over to them.'

Finally, they agreed that they could not go on without knowing exactly what lay ahead and that all they could do was to turn the cars around.

The Count asked Canali if he knew another place where they could take Mussolini. After thinking it over carefully, he suggested the house of the De Maria family at Bonzanigo di Mezzegra, a remote hamlet in the steep hills above the village of Azzano (which they had already driven through), three quarters of an hour's car journey away, where the couple had sheltered him several times. Alice Canali, sister of Luigi, later explained one of the reasons for her brother's decision: 'Lia De Maria was our foster sister. We had the same wet nurse. My brother knew that he could blindly trust her and her husband.'

The travellers set off along the road and told any partisans whom they had met previously at roadblocks that they had not been able to get to Como because of the fighting in the streets.

Mussolini showed no signs of surprise when he realised that the cars had turned around and did not ask why. He merely questioned how much farther they had to go and then chatted about the weather, saying that the rain would be good for the grain and grape harvests. Wrapping himself in a blanket, he seemed to doze off every so often, no longer a man of action, but one of life's passengers.

11 THE COUPLE'S LAST NIGHT

Mussolini and Petacci were brought back through rain and darkness to the lakeside village of Azzano. The two cars stopped at a crossroads and Canali told everyone to get out, as they had to walk for a few hundred metres using a short cut.

They set off up a narrow cobbled track between low stone walls. Canali and Moretti led the way, Mussolini and Petacci followed, and the Count, Tuissi, Cantoni, and Frangi brought up the rear.

A few minutes later, Mussolini asked if they could stop, as Petacci was tired. The couple were allowed to lean on the wall for a few moments, but when they set off again she experienced great difficulty in walking over the cobbles made slimy by the rain. The Count offered her his arm and the dictator did the same on the other side and they walked along in that way.

The Count recalled that they must have seemed a strange trio: Mussolini on the right, wearing a military cape that was too long for him, with a blanket over his shoulders and the white of his bandaged head standing out stark against the darkness of the night; an elegant lady in the middle, struggling along on high heels and weary with exhaustion; and on the left, the Count, threadbare and down-at-heel, with dishevelled hair and beard and clanking with all the weapons he was carrying.

After about quarter of an hour of slow walking the group came to the little hamlet of Bonzanigo.

Canali stopped at a wooden door and went into the yard of a large house overlooking the Via del Riale, home to 45-year-old workman Giacomo De Maria and his wife, Lia, who was 43.

He knocked at the door and few moments later Giacomo appeared. The two spoke together for a little while and then Canali called the others forward. They were led up a narrow stone staircase to the first floor and into a spacious kitchen, where Lia relit the log fire.

The prisoners were introduced as a couple of wounded Germans. Canali asked the family to look after them and to give them the best that the house could provide, adding that they would possibly stay for two or three days. Lia asked for a little time to prepare the bedroom upstairs in which their two teenage sons, Giovanni and Riccardo, were sleeping; they were hurriedly woken up and sent to stay in a mountain hut which the family owned.

Everyone sat around a large wooden table in the kitchen. Lia made a pot of ersatz coffee and they all drank it except Mussolini, who brusquely refused a cup. On the other hand, Petacci seemed grateful for it, cradling the vessel in her hands and beginning to relax in the warmth of the roaring fire.

The Count went upstairs with Canali and Moretti to take a look at the bedroom. It measured little more than three metres by three and a half metres. To the right of the door there was a small window. The Count looked out to see if it provided any opportunity for escape, but dismissed the thought after seeing that there was a drop of more than six metres to the ground.

Above the large double bed hung three modest paintings on a religious theme. In front of the wall opposite the window there was a small iron washbasin, while alongside it hung a faded photograph of a soldier in uniform, a cousin of Lia who had died during the First World War. A pair of wooden chairs completed the furniture in this small room with white walls.

Mussolini and Petacci did not have any suitcases with them, as they had been dumped together with those of the other Fascist leaders in the town hall at Dongo, and neither did they have many personal effects.

Petacci carried a scarf and a blue aviator's fur-lined cap, while Mussolini had the old grey Italian Army blanket given to him by Brigadier Giorgio Buffelli of the Finance Guards at Germasino, which was spread on the bed when Petacci said that she was cold.

Mussolini spoke little but asked for two pillows for himself and a comb for Petacci.

The Count told his two trusted partisans, Guglielmo Cantoni (Sandrino) and Giuseppe Frangi (Lino), that he was leaving them on guard and would send someone to relieve them as soon as possible. He ordered them to remain on the landing outside the couple's room and to go in at once if they heard anything suspicious, but not to disturb them unnecessarily. They were also told to avoid being seen by the neighbours in case they became suspicious at the presence of armed men in a peaceful house.

The De Marias became aware of the true identity of Mussolini at some point during the night, but had no idea who the pretty lady was.

Canali gave his last instructions to Giacomo as they prepared to leave. It was now after 5 a.m. on 28 April. Before closing the door, the Count took one last look at the prisoners. He recalled: 'They were sitting by the fire and I caught them in profile. Mussolini, his head still bandaged, was leaning back in his chair, with his hands in his lap and staring into the fire. Petacci was leaning forward slightly with her elbows on her knees and her chin resting on her hands.'

The Count intended to return to the house later on the same morning, or, if not, in the early afternoon. But, he was never to see the couple again.

12 PARTISAN PLOTS IN MILAN

While Mussolini spent the days of 25, 26 and 27 April 1945 desperately seeking a means of escape for himself and his followers, events in Milan changed from hour to hour in such a way as to eventually frustrate all his plans.

On the 25th, the underground Resistance leadership issued the order for the general rising. Its leaders were installed in a building in Via Brera, both from the political wing, the National Liberation Committee, and the military wing, the Corps of Volunteers of Liberty.

The insurrection began in earnest next day as rebel formations began to converge on the city from the remote areas in which they had been created.

The first of these to arrive, the Gramsci Division from the Oltrepò area of the province of Pavia, entered the city on the late afternoon of 27 April and made for the Piazzale Loreto, where fifteen partisans had been executed by the Fascists on 10 August 1944 as a reprisal. A fiery speech was made by Pietro Vergani (Fabio), Vice-Commandant of the military committee, who demanded the immediate capture and trial of Mussolini, followed by his public shooting in the square.

The division took over the elementary school in Viale Romagna, a large building with a spacious courtyard. In the evening the commanders visited their political and military leaders in Via Brera and received the news that Mussolini and the other senior Fascists had been captured in Dongo that afternoon.

Among the partisan commanders at the General Command were two men who would play a leading part in events that led to the executions: Aldo Lampredi (Guido Conti) and Walter Audisio (Colonel Valerio).

Lampredi was born in Florence on 13 March 1899. A cabinet

maker by trade, he became a labour activist and joined the Communist Party. In 1927 he was condemned to ten years and six months imprisonment by the Special Tribunal for Clandestine Activity. Lampredi was imprisoned in Civitavecchia and Pesaro, but gained his freedom in 1932 as the result of an amnesty. He crossed the border to France and later travelled to Russia.

On the outbreak of the Spanish Civil War, Lampredi was sent to serve in the commissariat of the International Brigades as an agent of *Comintern*, the international organisation that advocated Communism and whose agents were trained by the Soviet secret police. During 16 months following the September 1943 Armistice in Italy, he was appointed Inspector of the General Command of the Garibaldi Brigades, helped negotiate spheres of influence with the Yugoslav partisans, and organised armed resistance in Friuli and the Veneto.

At the beginning of 1945, Lampredi became an officer of the General Command of the military committee in Milan and the right-hand man of the Communist leader in the north, Luigi Longo.

Walter Audisio, an accountant at the family firm of Borsalino, famous hat makers, was born in Alessandria, Piedmont, on 28 June 1909. He joined the clandestine Communist Party in 1931, but was arrested by the Fascist secret police three years later and sentenced to confinement on the island of Ponza. In 1939, he petitioned Mussolini and was released 'as an act of clemency' on the grounds of poor health and the needs of his family.

In September 1943, Audisio began to organise the first partisan bands around Monferrato and afterwards commanded the Garibaldi Brigades operating in the province of Mantua and the lower Po area. As 'Colonel Valerio' he served as Inspector of the Garibaldi Brigades and in January 1945 was attached to the General Command of the military committee in Milan with responsibility for police work.

The new mission was initially entrusted to Aldo Lampredi, who immediately set about finding another leader to accompany him, as well as obtaining the necessary escort and transport. His first three choices of companion all refused to go, until finally Walter Audisio agreed to do so. At 10.30 p.m., he went with Lampredi and the leaders of the division to Viale Romagna to find twelve men for the task from among the partisans lodging in the school.

Two of the commanders making the selection would also become important participants in the events at Dongo: Alfredo Mordini (Riccardo) and Orfeo Landini (Piero), and both were known for their willingness to eliminate Fascists and Germans without remorse.

Mordini, a railwayman and a Communist since the early 1920s, had been arrested and confined on the island of Ventotene; after serving his sentence, he fled to France. Mordini then went on to take part in the great battles of the Spanish Civil War, where he was wounded, fought alongside the *Maquis* in France, and after the September 1943 Armistice in Italy became a partisan and Political Inspector of the 3rd Lombard Division Aliotta.

Landini, an industrial technician, served in North Africa as a Second-Lieutenant in the army in the 1930s and after coming into contact with the Communist Party was arrested in 1942 and sentenced to 18 years imprisonment for subversive activity. He was released in October 1943 following the Armistice, became a partisan in the Oltrepò Pavese area, and was appointed Political Commissar of the Aliotta Division in the autumn of 1944.

In January 1945, Landini was captured by the Germans and imprisoned at Novi Ligure, but after making a daring escape he regained his freedom and was given responsibility for the intelligence and police service of the division, which was manned by the best men from each detachment.

Mordini was appointed commander of the escort leaving for

Dongo and Landini accompanied him as his lieutenant. Arguably, the least suited to the mission was Audisio. Referring to his past occupation as an accountant at the hat factory, the Communist deputy Celeste Negarville said later that he was: 'More suited to measuring a head than cutting it off.' Though Audisio did have previous military experience as an officer cadet, many of his companions would say later that in contrast to Mordini and Landini he was better qualified to planning the mission than to carrying it out.

Audisio had spent the time since he arrived at the Viale Romagna in going to and fro between there and Via Brera to obtain the documents and permits necessary to pass the partisan roadblocks on the journey and in finding transport for the escort.

He first obtained a pass for the mission from General Cadorna.

It read:

The bearer of this document, with the identity card of the municipality of Milan number 274,095 made out to Giovan Battista Magnoli di Cesare, is directly answerable to this command with the task of liaison. Therefore, all formations belonging to the CVL are invited to facilitate him in every exercise of his functions. The holder of this document is Colonel Valerio of this command.

Audisio also procured another pass with the signature of an American Captain by the use of guile. Emilio (Mim) Daddario, agent 774 of the United States OSS Secret Intelligence (SI) detachment, had reached Milan and made contact with General Cadorna as an Allied officer officially accredited to the National Liberation Committee. He was asked to sign numerous documents of this type, but was not aware that Audisio wanted to execute Mussolini or that Lampredi was going along with him.

But though Audisio was a very determined man and a member of a highly disciplined party, it seems that he was far from the bloodthirsty avenger portrayed by the Communists, as at the last minute he tried to outsource the task to another formation: the highly regarded Finance Guards. Former commander of the Milan legion, Colonel Alfredo Malgeri, recalled that he was in the Prefecture on the late afternoon of 27 April when a young guard suddenly arrived from the Como area and announced that Mussolini had been arrested.

The Colonel immediately informed the military committee and in the evening was summoned to their command in Via Brera. The information was still vague and imprecise and yet from that moment steps were being taken to carry out the deadly wishes of hardliners on the committee.

Malgeri found Audisio waiting for him and they had a conversation along these lines:

'Colonel,' he said, 'we are going to entrust you with a mission, following which you can request and receive any reward or promotion you would like. It is a mission of the greatest delicacy, for which we believe that you are especially suited. You have to go and pick up Mussolini with the means you deem appropriate to transport him to Milan. Of course, you know better than me how such things can end up. Captives normally try to escape and it is logical that they should do so. It follows that these assignments lead to the death of those who try to escape.

'I'm now letting you know that the General Command would see nothing wrong in an outcome of this type to your mission, especially since, as you know, there is also the danger that Mussolini might fall into the hands of the Allies alive. Therefore, as I repeat, such a solution would not be unwelcome to the Command; indeed, all of us would be very grateful to you.' [1]

Malgeri related: 'I was very tired, I answered without committing myself. I didn't have a precise knowledge of the situation, which I reserved the right to clarify.' He returned to the barracks and telephoned several headquarters in the Como area in a vain attempt to find any news. Meanwhile, the Colonel recalled: 'The phone calls from Valerio followed me one after another. I made him understand that I didn't think I could carry out the mission.'

At 10.30 p.m., Malgeri received the first reliable information in a phonogram from Lieutenant-Colonel Luigi Villani of the Finance Guards in Menaggio, saying that Mussolini had been arrested by the 52nd Garibaldi Brigade and was being held in the Germasino barracks.

In the meantime, Colonel Malgeri had been consulting his subordinates. Brigadier Vincenzo Dell'Acqua said he opposed the idea of bringing Mussolini to Milan, as 'the Finance Guards have nothing to do with political parties and other entities.' Together with Lieutenant Giorgio Ognibene, he then refused to take part, saying they had clean hands and did not intend to stain them with blood. On their reply, the Colonel said: 'I too am of the same opinion,' after which he went with Dell' Acqua to telephone Audisio, who replied: 'Very well, I will deal with the matter myself.'

A Fiat 1100 car and a small open-body diesel pickup truck of the West Ticino Society were requisitioned by the party. The partisan platoon, all with new khaki uniforms and submachine guns from recent Anglo-American airdrops, climbed onto the truck with their inspector, Landini, while Lampredi, Audisio, and Mordini were driven in the Fiat.

The group left Milan on their fateful mission just after six in the morning, initial destination Como.

13 COLONEL VALERIO

It was already daylight when the Count got back to Dongo after leaving Mussolini and Petacci as prisoners in the house in Bonzanigo. He was tired out, but could not find time to rest, as he had urgent administrative matters to deal with.

Everything was going smoothly until shortly after 1.30 p.m. a courier brought an urgent message that had been received from Menaggio by the telephone exchange.

Two vehicles had refused to stop and crashed through a partisan roadblock of stones and tree trunks at full speed towards the upper lake. One was a car with a Rome registration number, RM 001, and the other was a lorry full of armed men; they were suspected of being Fascists and the brigade commanders were warned to be on the lookout.

The messenger was still talking when a partisan rushed in to report that the lorry had just arrived in the town square. The men had got out and taken up positions in front of the town hall and their officer had demanded to see the local commander.

This man, presenting himself as Colonel Valerio, had arrived in Como with his men at around eight o'clock on the wet morning of 28 April and gone to meet the National Liberation Committee, which was largely composed of moderate elements and had just occupied the Prefecture. Addressing the new partisan commander of the zone, Lieutenant-Colonel Baron Giovanni Sardagna of Hohenstein, and the new Prefect, Virginio Bertinelli, he requested a truck large enough to carry the prisoners and the escort back to Milan. At the same time, Lampredi and Mordini went to the Communist headquarters to try to obtain news of the whereabouts of Mussolini and his followers.

Valerio told the committee that he had arrived from Milan on a secret mission on behalf of General Cadorna, Commander-in-Chief of the military committee. The Colonel carried himself with an air of authority. He was described as approaching forty, rather tall and dark, with a long, angular face, and distinctive features; he wore a partisan uniform of a brick colour and his only marks of rank were three stars on a red shield of cloth sown on the left hand side of his tunic.

Valerio's credentials were examined by a member of the Liberation Committee and found to be in order. Soon afterwards, a meeting was convened to discuss what should be done with Mussolini and his followers, whose capture at Dongo had been known since the previous night. The members of the Committee avoided giving a direct answer, as they did not want to give up their prisoners, seeing that their own men had captured them and would be unwilling to hand them over to any other partisan unit.

It was finally agreed that Mussolini would be transported to Milan and entrusted to General Cadorna with the request that he be placed at the disposition of the Allied authorities. However, after four hours of discussion Valerio was only promised two cars and an ambulance (in which Mussolini would be hidden) on condition that the little convoy would be accompanied by two prominent members of the local movement: Major Cosimo Maria De Angelis, leader of the Military Committee, and Oscar Sforni, textile worker and General Secretary of the Liberation Committee. Their only aim was to frustrate Valerio's scheme by taking over Mussolini themselves and bringing him to Como, where a cell had already been prepared in the prison of San Donnino.

Valerio asked to use the telephone and got through to his leader, Luigi Longo, who was waiting for news in the secret base for the publication of the party's underground newspaper *Unità* in Via Solferino, Milan. All Longo could hear at first were several people shouting and then Valerio came on the line, also shouting: 'The Como National Liberation Committee is more terrified than honoured by the capture of Mussolini,' he said. 'They are trying to put a spoke in the wheel and I'm unable to find out where he and the other leaders are being held. What shall I do?'

Longo cut him short and snapped: 'Either kill him, or you will be killed.' Following the telephone call, Valerio become very impatient and brusquely ordered everyone to leave the room. According to Sforni he was waving his machine gun around while he spoke and gave orders.

When the two Como partisan leaders went outside the Prefecture with him he appeared nervous and standoffish and told them to find a lorry in which to transport his men to Dongo. The idea of sending a motorised column had seemingly been abandoned.

By chance, Valerio saw a large covered furniture lorry, yellow in colour, passing at that very moment and commandeered it at gunpoint. He ejected the driver and his mate, loaded his men on board, and told Sforni and De Angelis to lead the way in their Lancia Aprile.

When leaving Como, the Colonel learned with amazement that Lampredi and Mordini had gone to Dongo before him. It was said that they had done so fearing that Mussolini might be captured by an Allied mission, but, after seeing that that he was being held under strict surveillance, were content to await the arrival of the main party. This occurred at around 2.10 p.m. after breaking through the roadblock outside Menaggio.

Valerio and his men were initially greeted by the raised guns of the local partisans. He related that the atmosphere was cold and hostile due to the unexpected arrival of Sforni and De Angelis in a suspect black car and by their excited report that something suspicious was afoot. The pair asked Valerio what they should do, only to be told that their role was simply to witness events.

One of the Colonel's lieutenants, Orfeo Landini (Piero), recalled that they had driven along the lakeside road at speed, often skidding around the many corners and not thinking they would meet any obstacles.

However, at Menaggio the vehicle crashed through the road block of stones and tree trunks as if it were an armoured car and the occupants only learned later that the local partisans had shouted at them to stop and fired shots after them. When the party reached the square in Dongo there was an atmosphere of suspicion everywhere and every face looked at them with distrust.

Landini was struck by the appearance of the local partisans, relating: 'They reminded me a little of the early days of partisan warfare when our uniforms were not in fact uniforms at all, when we had long beards and dishevelled hair, looking like a cross between a soldier and a hill peasant and suggesting rather a soldier of fortune than an enlisted man.'

Valerio was unable to get his documents recognised by Brigadier of the Finance Guards Giorgio Buffelli, who would not even give him a hearing, so he sternly rebuked him for treating a senior officer in this way and referred him to the rules of military discipline. The partisan on guard at the town hall entrance also stubbornly refused to let him in or to listen to what he had to say, though finally, after some sharp and energetic exchanges, he was persuaded to send for his commanding officer.

To gain time, the Count sent a message to the new arrival that he was waiting in his office and that he could come up at once. A few minutes later the partisan returned and said that the officer had flown into a rage when he received the request and threatened to arrest everyone if his orders were not carried out. He said that he was from General Headquarters and had been sent with full powers; in view of this he was ordering the local commander to come to him. The Count decided to go down, reflecting that it was useless trying to gain more time and that it was better to face the situation at once.

He went out into the square. It was deserted except for a line of fifteen men drawn up in perfect military formation about 20 metres from the town hall. They all wore brand new uniforms and were armed with submachine guns. Standing a few yards in front of the platoon was their officer.

The Count introduced himself as the commander of the 52nd Brigade and the man said that he was Colonel Valerio, the special envoy from the General Headquarters of the Corps of Volunteers of Liberty.

'I need to speak to you in private on matters of the greatest importance,' he said.

'Well, come along to my office,' the Count replied. 'We will not be disturbed there. Leave your men here and follow me.'

However, Valerio insisted that they went with him everywhere and set off for the entrance to the town hall, waving them to follow. The Count asked them: 'Are you hungry?' A chorus of famished voices affirmed that they were and he diverted them to the cookhouse, while he took the Colonel up to his office, unfastening the top of his holster just in case of trouble.

Sforni and De Angelis were left stranded in the square. After waiting in vain for half an hour for an invitation to the meeting, De Angelis entered the town hall and said that in the circumstances they had no alternative but to return to Como.

Valerio immediately ordered their arrest. As they had left Como in a hurry, there had been no time to prepare any credentials, and since they were largely unknown in Dongo it was only too easy for him to order this action. They were surrounded by local partisans and marched off to a cell with their hands in the air and machine guns at their back. Sforni wrote later: 'Owing to Colonel Valerio, the new democratic order began with a resounding episode of violence and abuse.' On his orders, the pair were only released two hours after his departure.

The Count was slightly delayed as he stopped to talk to some of his men and as he walked along the corridor leading to the little room that had been set aside as his office he saw Valerio talking to another person. This was Aldo Lampredi (Guido Conti), described by the Count as a strange man who always stayed in the background and of whom very little was known. However, Canali had met Lampredi before and was able to vouch for him. The Count heard Valerio saying to his companion: 'Our own personal problems don't enter into it. We'll see about those later. I'm here to carry out my task and I won't have any interference.'

The Count led the pair into his office and sat down at his desk, with the Colonel facing him and Lampredi leaning against a small table. 'First of all, my credentials,' Valerio said, taking two sheets of paper out of his pocket and handing them to the Count. He recalled: 'Both seemed perfectly authentic and it seemed beyond doubt that he was our superior officer sent by General Headquarters with full powers and that we must obey him.'

He handed back the documents and said: 'All right. Well, what is it you want?'

The Colonel responded: 'You've arrested Mussolini and several of his ministers, isn't that so? Then you are to hand them over to me.'

The Count replied: 'The 52nd Brigade captured them and it seems only right that we should be the ones to transfer them to the headquarters.'

But Valerio snapped: 'There's no question of that. I've come to shoot them, these are my orders, shoot the lot.'

The Count was dumfounded and just managed to stammer: 'What? But we can't shoot them like that, summarily, without a sentence. But...'

The Colonel interrupted him: 'The sentence has been passed by the National Liberation Committee and it is an order from General Headquarters. I am charged with carrying out that order and I intend to do so. You are only a subordinate and I am your superior officer.

Your only duty is to obey. Let that be quite clear. There can be no discussion. Bring me the nominal roll.'

The Count asked to be able to consult Canali, Moretti, and Tuissi, who were in the next room. They were also perplexed and irritated on hearing the news, but finally they all decided that there was no alternative but to obey, though they would point out that they did so with the greatest reluctance and disapproval. Then they traipsed into the office. Valerio said: 'Well, what have you decided?'

'We will hand the prisoners over to you,' the Count replied. 'But as we are all against what you have decided to do we will hand them over and that is all. The rest is for you to decide.'

'Excellent,' he retorted. 'Mine was the order and mine is the responsibility. Give me the nominal roll.'

He had not known exactly who the partisans had captured, but immediately began to put a single black cross in the right-hand margin against many of the names.

'Benito Mussolini, death … Claretta Petacci, death...'

'You'll shoot Petacci,' the Count exclaimed in horror. 'What, you'll shoot a woman? She's not to blame.'

'She was Mussolini's advisor and she's been behind his policies for all these years. She's just as much responsible as he is.'

'Advisor, my foot,' said the Count. 'She was nothing but his mistress. To condemn her for that…'

'It is not I who am condemning her. Judgement has already been passed,' snarled Valerio. 'Remember that I am carrying out an order and you are not to interfere. I know what I'm doing and I'm the one to decide.'

He went on reading through the list of prisoners, and there was an argument against nearly every name, but he was determined and chose fifteen people for execution. As he made clear later, this was a decision that he had already made before leaving Milan so as to match the number of partisans the Germans had ordered the Fascists to execute in Piazzale Loreto, Milan, on 10 August 1944, forbidding their families from retrieving their bodies for the entire day. The list of the names of the prisoners for execution was hand-written on two scraps of paper and signed using the aliases: 'MAGNOLI '(in capitals), and 'Guido Conti.'

When he had finished, Valerio asked if there were any other prisoners. The Count told him about the Spaniard they had arrested and ordered him to be brought immediately from the Dongo Hotel. While they were waiting, the Colonel was told that the prisoners had been divided into three groups: Mussolini and Petacci were in a place half way along the shore of the lake; Barracu, Bombacci, Casalinuovo, Pavolini, Porta, and Utimpergher in Germasino; and Calistri, Coppola, Daquanno, Gatti, Liverani, Romano, Nudi, Mezzasoma, and Zerbino in Dongo.

Valerio kept on repeating that he was in a hurry and had to be back in Milan with the bodies before nightfall. The Count recalled that his concern was the opposite: he wanted to gain time in the vain hope that something or other might turn up to prevent him from completing his mission. Though he was now convinced that he could not oppose his orders and agreed that the prisoners had to face up to their responsibilities, he would have preferred their sentences to come from a properly constituted court, rather than acting in a manner that resembled the practices of the Fascists themselves.

Still to gain time, the Count decided that he would fetch the prisoners from Germasino while Canali and Moretti collected Mussolini and Petacci. He wrote later: 'They would all then be in Dongo, where they could be handed over to Valerio and executed.'

The Count went back to Germasino in a Fiat 2800 driven by Hofmann, with four partisans following in another vehicle. The prisoners were brought out and loaded into the two cars. The Count took Barracu, Casalinuovo, Pavolini, Porta and a partisan in his car, while he put Bombacci and Utimpergher in the second vehicle.

As they drove along, the prisoners talked among themselves and did not appear to be giving any thought to what fate might hold in store for them.

In Dongo meanwhile, Marcello Petacci had been brought to the Count's office, where Lazzaro was pointing out the inaccuracies in the family's passports to Valerio. He addressed the suspect in basic Spanish and when he discovered that he could not even speak the language, leapt to his feet, and gave him a tremendous slap across the face.

The Colonel seized a pistol and shouted at him: 'Stick your hands up, you rat; come on get them up, or I'll kill you. I know who you are, you swine, you're Vittorio Mussolini.'

The Count, Lazzaro, and Lampredi were awestruck at the sudden change of atmosphere and simply stood and stared. The man lowered his arms, took a step towards Valerio, and stuttered: 'You're making a terrible mistake, I'm warning you. I am not Vittorio Mussolini, I am Don Juan y Muñez…'

'Silence,' the Colonel shouted, waving the revolver in his face.

'Bill, take this man outside and shoot him at once.'

Lazzaro reluctantly took his gun from its holster and ordered the prisoner to go in front of him with his hands up. They went down the stairs and out into the square. As the man was still loudly protesting his innocence, Lazzaro found some partisans to escort him to an isolated place where he could be shot.

Someone suggested the grounds of the Capuchin monastery and the others agreed. One of them asked: 'Who is he?'

'Vittorio Mussolini,' Lazzaro replied casually, and a crowd began to gather and to hurl threats and insults at the wretched man. As he continued to plead for his life, they reached the monastery wall and one of the holy fathers was summoned at his request.

The guards were told to move ten metres or so away to give the pair some privacy and Lazzaro told the prisoner: 'It is three o' clock.

I give you half an hour. I warn you that any attempt to escape will be futile, as you can see if you look around you.' The priest knelt down on the ground near the condemned man and began to write in a little notebook at his dictation.

'Only two minutes left ... one ... that's it, your times up,' Lazzaro called. The father wrote a few more words down and then got up and came to him, followed by the prisoner who had a gleam of hope in his eyes.

'I beg you to grant him a few moments longer to explain some facts of the greatest importance,' said the priest.

'All right. I am not the Spanish Consul, but I am not Vittorio Mussolini either,' said the man. 'I am Marcello Petacci.'

At first, Lazzaro did not attach any significance to the name, but suddenly the penny dropped and he realised that he was talking to Claretta's brother. The priest nodded his head to confirm this.

The partisan asked for proof and the suspect said that they would find a briefcase and a letter addressed to him in his hotel room. Lazzaro borrowed a bicycle and pedalled there at high speed.

In the room he found a woman whom he believed to be Petacci's wife and two local women who ushered the children out. Lazzaro looked for the letter, but it had disappeared.

The lady burst into tears and revealed that Marcello was not actually her husband but her partner and that her name was Zita Ritossa. Taken aback, Lazzaro reassured her and said that the letter would have been useful, but in its absence the briefcase would be adequate. She handed it over and he swiftly returned to the priest and the prisoner. The briefcase was opened and revealed a set of technical drawings and several documents addressed to Marcello Petacci. 'All right,' said Lazzaro, and ordered his men to take him back to the town hall.

The Count had just arrived in the square with the prisoners he had collected from Germasino. Lazzaro told him that the prisoner whom

Valerio had taken to be Vittorio Mussolini was in fact Marcello Petacci and that he should not be shot. A local partisan who knew the dictator's son also intervened to confirm that he was not the man claiming to be the Spanish Consul.

'You're quite right, Bill. We'll tell Valerio when he gets back,' said the Count.

'What? Isn't he here then?'

'Not on your life. He's gone with Moretti and Canali to fetch Mussolini and Petacci while I went to Germasino for the prisoners.'

At that moment a partisan escort had just brought a relieved Marcello Petacci to the square and he glimpsed the Count's car carrying Barracu, Casalinuovo, Pavolini, and Porta and told Lazzaro that they could vouch for his identity.

Petacci waved to them, but as soon as they saw him, they looked away. Lazzaro demanded: 'Do you know this man?' They all said no, and the shocked prisoner was marched back to the hotel.

After returning to Dongo and witnessing the strange episode of Marcello Petacci calling out to the prisoners, the Count sent them up to the Golden Room of the town hall.

As he went out into the square he saw that Valerio had just arrived. He was in a state of great excitement and came up to him yelling: 'Justice is done. Mussolini is dead.'

'What? But I thought we had agreed…'

'I know, I know, but I couldn't waste any more time. It's getting late and I had already lost several precious hours. Where are the others? Have you collected them?'

Writing later, the Count said that he had realised that there was nothing more to be done; they had to bow to the inevitable. The Colonel did not give him any details of the execution, but Moretti showed him the MAS-38 submachine gun captured during the Gravedona mission a month earlier, and said: 'This was the weapon that killed the tyrant.'

The Count took Valerio to see the prisoners. On the landing of the town hall they met Doctor Giuseppe Rubini, the new Mayor, who had heard of his intentions and was angry that the shooting was going to take place in the middle of a crowd of people that included women and children.

The doctor said: 'We detest the Nazis and Fascists for their barbarism, don't we? I forbid this execution. If you ignore me I shall resign my position and leave it to public opinion to judge.'

Valerio shrugged and snapped: 'All right, if you're too sensitive, don't come,' and turned his back on him.

Rubini went to the window, lowered the Italian flag in disgust, went home, and wrote out his resignation letter as the executions were about to begin.

14 THE COUPLE'S LAST DAY

Saturday, 28 April had dawned wet and humid, with a light breeze causing gentle ripples on the lake. In their household prison in the hamlet of Bonzanigo, Mussolini and Petacci slept on until midday.

After getting up, she asked for some polenta and a little milk. Lia took two portions to the bedroom, together with a plate of home-made salami and rationed bread. Petacci ate heartily, while Mussolini only tried two slices of the salami and a little bread. He did not drink the milk, only a few sips of water - just as he had refused the coffee the night before - perhaps fearing being poisoned.

The rest of the meal would remain in the room for several days after their departure. A piece of partially-used wartime soap, which had evidently been carried by the couple, was left on the washbasin. Also found in the room was the leather airman's cap belonging to Petacci and a pair of blue militia trousers, which Mussolini must have worn or carried with him.

According to Giacomo, the dictator seemed rested and rejuvenated after having slept and washed, but did not shave; he continued to say little and appeared sad, to all questions replying 'Fine, fine' in a monotonous voice.

Giacomo later told Canali of the mysterious disappearance of one of their old knives, which had been on the table in the kitchen on the arrival of their unexpected guests during the night. He said that he was certain that Mussolini had taken it when he found himself alongside the table. This raises a variety of questions on his intentions at that perilous time, but, whatever they were, the knife was found in the bedroom occupied by the couple after their departure.

Lia remained at home all day and got on with her household chores, while Giacomo worked outside and then wandered into the hamlet. The news that Mussolini had travelled along the road below the houses on the previous afternoon had spread like wildfire, but the workman did not say a word about his guests, and their presence remained a secret. This was even the case after the arrival of an unwelcome visitor at the house, who reported that American troops had reached Como. Shortly afterwards, Mussolini opened the door of his bedroom to ask if this was true and on receiving a positive reply appeared visibly shaken by the news, fearing that his nightmare of capture and trial could soon become a reality.

Around four in the afternoon, the sound of heavy footsteps was heard and Moretti arrived with two strangers: Colonel Valerio, whom Lia described as rather tall, with his hair combed back, and wearing a light raincoat and a cap, and Guido Conti, the major political figure of the mission, who spoke with the soft tones of his native Tuscany.

Giacomo escorted the Colonel to the room above and remained outside. After knocking, Valerio went in. Through the closed door, the workman heard him telling Mussolini and Petacci that they must leave with him immediately, repeating several times that there was no time to lose. Within the space of a few minutes the couple had left the house. Lia watched them go through the gate from an upstairs window and went into the bedroom. The pillows were stained with mascara.

Pallid and crying, Petacci gripped Mussolini's arm, and he reassured her and hugged her to him.

What happened next would be made public two days later in an article in the Milanese edition of *Unità*, the official newspaper of the Italian Communist Party.

Reliable sources soon indicated that the author of the piece was indeed 'Colonel Valerio.' The article opens the next chapter.

15 THE EXECUTION

The Communist version of the executions in *Unità* read:

The Partisan who Executed '*Il Duce*' Speaks:
'I Fired Five Shots at Mussolini from a Distance of Three Paces'

We have had the good fortune to speak to the executor of Mussolini's death sentence. In a few words he told us briefly about the inglorious end of a man who at the cost of any shame has left to history his vile comments, his fear, and his poor attachment to life.

Aware of the importance of the prisoners they had captured, the command of the 52nd Brigade Luigi Clerici divided them up into three groups. Mussolini and Petacci had been taken to the locality of Mezzegra (Tremezzina) in the province of Como and guarded in a room without windows in a peasant house halfway up the hill. [1]

I entered the room with the machine gun levelled. Mussolini was standing by the bed. He was wearing a dark brown coat and the cap of the GNR without insignia, while his boots were laced at the back. His gaze was lost in the void, his eyes were out of their sockets, his lower lip trembled, and he was a terrified man. The first words he uttered were: 'What's going on?'

I had planned to execute him in a place not far from the house. To lead him there, I had to use a trick. I replied: 'I've come to free you.'

'Truly?'

'Quickly, quickly, we must move. There's no time to lose…'

'Where are we going?'

With the intonation of someone who wanted to offer him a weapon, I asked him: 'Are you armed?'

'No, I don't have weapons,' he replied, with the tone of someone who had understood the situation.

Mussolini moved to go out, but I stopped him: 'First, the lady.'

Petacci did not understand what was happening, but rapidly collected her personal effects.

'Quickly, move...'

At this point, Mussolini set off, because he could not wait any longer. In fact, he went out before Petacci. As soon as he was outside he changed his attitude and, turning to me, said: 'I offer you an empire.' We were still in the doorway. Instead of replying, I said to Petacci: 'Let's go, let's go,' and I pushed her out with one arm. Petacci caught up with Mussolini and the pair followed me. We took the path from the house to the place where a car was waiting.

While he was walking, Mussolini gave me a grateful glance. I whispered to him: 'I've also freed your son, Vittorio.' From his reply, I wanted to find out where Vittorio was to be found.

'Heartfelt thanks.'

He then asked: 'And where are Zerbino and Mezzasoma?'

'We're also freeing them,' I replied.

'Ah ...,' and he did not turn again.

When we reached the car, Mussolini seemed convinced that he was a free man. He made a gesture as if to let Petacci climb in first, but I said to him: 'You get in. You'll be safer. Even though that Fascist cap might create some problems...'

Mussolini took it off and, rubbing his head with one hand, exclaimed: 'And this?'

'Well then, lower the beret to above your eyes...'

We set off. When we reached the place I had chosen earlier - a curve on the right hand side of the road, with a low wall on the left that ran as far as a layby - I ordered the car to stop. I gestured to Mussolini not to talk. Approaching the door, I whispered to him: 'I've heard some noises ... I'm going to see ...' I got out of the car and headed for the curve. Then I went back and whispered again: 'Quickly, go to that corner.'

Although he obeyed promptly, Mussolini did not seem so certain any longer. He placed himself with his shoulders against the wall, as ordered, Petacci on his right. Silence.

Suddenly, I pronounced the sentence for war criminals: 'On the orders of the General Command of the Corps of Volunteers of Liberty, I have been ordered to obtain justice for the Italian people.' Mussolini seemed dazed. Petacci threw her arms around his neck and said: 'He must not die.'

'Go back to your place, if you don't want to die too.'

The woman backed away. At a distance of three paces, I fired five times at Mussolini, who fell to his knees with his head resting on his chest. Then it was the turn of Petacci. Justice was done.

The sensational report of almost seven hundred words had already been written when a hasty autopsy began to be carried out on Mussolini in Milan and so the journalists could not take into account its conclusion that he had been hit by at least eight bullets. [2]

Further newspaper accounts followed. Editor of the *Corriere d'Informazione*, Ferruccio Lanfranchi, wrote a series of eleven articles headlined 'Investigation into the Events of Dongo,' which appeared between 20 October and 2 November 1945. His work prompted the publication of twenty-four anonymous articles in the Rome edition of *Unità* in November and December, entitled 'How I killed Mussolini,' with a preface by Luigi Longo, then the Communist Party's Vice-Secretary.

The articles added some minor details that seem to have been the product of a journalist's imagination but also contained two major claims: that the submachine gun fired by Colonel Valerio had jammed, and that he had not acted alone, but with the assistance of two other partisans, who were identified as Guido and Bill, the aliases of Aldo Lampredi and Urbano Lazzaro.

The presence of Lazzaro at Bonzanigo was contradicted in an

article he wrote shortly afterwards with the Count for the local newspaper, the *Corriere Lombardo*, which named two others as the companions of the Colonel: Luigi Canali (Captain Neri) and Alfredo Mordini (Riccardo), commander of the execution squad at Dongo.

The revelation that 'Colonel Valerio' was actually the accountant Walter Audisio from Alessandria was made for the first time by his political enemies (and not his friends) in a series of anonymous articles in a Milanese neo-fascist publication, the *Meridiano d'Italia*, in February and March 1947; in them, he was described not as an executioner but as a murderer.

On 3 March, Audisio gave an interview to Radio Switzerland in which he admitted to having killed Mussolini, and this was confirmed in *Unità* on the 22nd and by the Communist Party in a communiqué next day. Three days later, the newspaper began to publish a series of six articles entitled 'Colonel Valerio Speaks,' which were signed by Walter Audisio. Once again, minor details differed from those published previously. On the 28th, he was officially presented to the public during a Communist rally at the Massenzio basilica in Rome, which was attended by forty thousand people.

Audisio was subsequently elected to represent the Communist Party in parliament, three times as a Deputy and once as a Senator, which partially protected him from judicial investigations. He died in Rome on 11 October 1973, but his memoir, *In nome del popolo italiano* (In the Name of the Italian People), was published two years later.

According to this final version, Moretti and Lampredi were sent to block the road in both directions. Audisio read the sentence of death for war criminals and told Petacci, who was clinging to Mussolini, 'Get out of the way if you don't want to die too.' She let go. Audisio pressed the trigger, but the submachine gun jammed. In his turn, Lampredi tried to fire with a pistol, but this also jammed. Audisio called Moretti, who rushed to bring him his submachine gun. After berating Mussolini, who was frozen by fear, Audisio fired a burst of five shots at him, which also killed Petacci, who, frantic and dazed, had moved confusedly, was hit and fell to the ground on all fours. Finally, a coup de grace was exploded into Mussolini's heart, without the weapon being specified, possibly Lampredi's pistol, which this time did not misfire, though, as we shall see, several reports said that Audisio had one too.

The Thompson submachine gun he first tried to use had been given to him by Alberto Mario Cavallotti, the Political Commissar of the 3rd Garibaldi Division Lombardia Aliotta, when they were choosing the men for the mission in the school in Milan on the previous evening.

The weapon had arrived in an American airdrop days earlier, but no one had removed the protective fat inside and so it did not fire. Some time later, Valerio returned the submachine gun to Cavallotti without it ever being used.

Lampredi was armed with a 1934 model Beretta pistol, calibre 9 mm, number 778133. On returning to Dongo, he gave it to Alfredo Mordini (Riccardo) 'to commemorate the execution of the *Duce*.' When Mordini died in 1969 his widow passed it on to Piero Boveri, a former partisan from Varzi, who in his turn donated it to the Historical Museum of Voghera in 1983.

Moretti had a French MAS-38 submachine gun, calibre 7.65 long, number F 20830, which had a red ribbon tied to the top of the barrel. The weapon was seized in the partisan attack of 29 March 1945 on the Hotel Turismo in Gravedona, which was frequented by Fascists and Germans; Captain Giacomo Valenti, commander of the frontier force, fell victim during the clash and his gun was taken by Moretti.

On 30 November 1957, Audisio donated the weapon to his 'Dear Comrades of the Albanian Communist Party' on the thirtieth anniversary of their country's liberation, writing: 'It was the weapon with which - on 28 April 1945 - the war criminal Benito Mussolini was executed on the orders of the General Command of the Italian partisans.' The submachine gun is now conserved in the Museum of Tirana in Albania.

In several interviews, Audisio's cousin, Franca De Tomasi, revealed the origin of the first article that appeared in *Unità*. At the time she was a typist for the central military committee and recalled that she transcribed the report on 29 April 1945, the day after the killings. Using the cover name of Colonel Valerio, Audiso made his statement consulting sheets of notes written by Lampredi, every so often stopping to ask him to approve a phrase. At the end of the dictation, Lampredi turned to Audisio and said: 'We're in agreement then. From this moment you take on the role of hero,' adding to De Tomasi: 'This is the version that must be handed down to history. Is that clear?'

The Communist leaders tried to manage the story for a variety of reasons. They were wedded to secrecy after more than 20 years as members of an underground organisation; there were concerns that neo-fascists might seek revenge; and it was well known that there were many aspects of the episode that it was preferable not to advertise.

Above all, the Communists tried to portray the shootings as the expression of the spontaneous revolt of the Italian people against Fascism and suggested that it was not important to know who materially carried it out. In this way they also hoped to avoid having to answer any secondary questions.

This also suited the British and the Americans, both of whom had their secret agents on the ground throughout April 1945, as we shall see in the following chapters.

16 MORE KILLINGS

Colonel Valerio quickly returned to Dongo after executing Mussolini and Petacci at Giulino di Mezzegra, arriving back just before five in the afternoon and putting preparations in hand for the shooting of the remaining prisoners chosen earlier.

Soon afterwards, Accursio Ferrari, one of the fathers from the nearby Capuchin monastery (the Sanctuary of the Madonna delle Lacrime) arrived after rumours had swept the town that the men captured the day before were about to be executed. He asked Valerio for permission to give them the sacrament of Extreme Unction, which allows absolution without repentance in certain emergency situations. The Colonel replied that only three minutes would be allowed owing to urgent military needs. The father protested that this was insufficient time to minister to so many men, but Valerio replied that there was no alternative and invited him to follow him to the place of execution in the Piazza Filippo Lillia.

The prisoners were brought down to the courtyard of the town hall and roll call took place. It was then announced that they were sentenced to be shot in the back as traitors. The 52nd Brigade's commanders agreed that the men would be marched out in Indian file, each flanked by one of their partisans, and would then be handed over at the place appointed for the execution, a small parapet running alongside the square by the side of the lake. The local men would leave and Valerio's squad would take over.

However, he had other ideas and demanded that the firing squad should be composed of half of his own men and half of the brigade's men, but the Count refused, saying that he had to hand the prisoners over, but would not order anyone to take part in the execution. In addition, to show his disapproval, he would withdraw from the square. Valerio flew into a rage and commanded him to stay put, which he did reluctantly.

Just as they had finished talking, the prisoners emerged from the town hall. They marched slowly, each one with an armed partisan by his side, crossed the square, and reached the lakeside.

They were lined up along the parapet, the escort withdrew and the firing squad took over, standing in line four or five metres from the condemned men. Each partisan was armed with a submachine gun and had one prisoner facing him.

The Fascists were:

Colonel Francesco Maria Barracu, Under-Secretary to the Presidency of the Council
Nicola Bombacci, friend of Mussolini and one of the founders of the Italian Communist Party in 1921
Captain Pietro Calistri, air force officer
Colonel Vito Casalinuovo, liaison officer between Mussolini and the National Republican Guard
Goffredo Coppola, Rector of the University of Bologna and President of the Fascist Institute of Culture
Ernesto Daquanno, director of the Stefani Press Agency
Prefect Luigi Gatti, private secretary of Mussolini
Augusto Liverani, Minister of Post and Communications
Fernando Mezzasoma, Minister of Popular Culture
Mario Nudi, commandant of Mussolini's musketeers
Alessandro Pavolini, National Secretary of the Fascist Republican Party
Paolo Porta, lawyer, federal commissar of Como and commander of the XI Black Brigade Cesare Rodini of Como
Ruggero Romano, Minister of Public Works
Idreno Utimpergher, commander of the XXVI Black Brigade Natale Piacentini of Lucca
Paolo Zerbino, Minister of the Interior

Father Accursio Ferrari stepped forward and spoke a few words of comfort to the men and gave them the general absolution. While he was doing this, Valerio suddenly remembered the suspect Spaniard and asked the Count what had happened to him; when told that he was really Marcello Petacci and had been brought back to the town hall, he ordered that he be sent for and shot with the rest.

Petacci was taken to the square and marched towards the row of prisoners. However, when they saw him a confused shouting arose from them to the effect that he was a traitor and should not be shot with them.

Valerio yelled in a rage: 'Forward. Put him with the others, finish him off!' The Count intervened and said that it would make no difference if Petacci was shot alone and that condemned men were usually allowed one last request. The Colonel reluctantly gave in. Petacci was led to one side and the other prisoners quietened down and stood in line again.

Alfredo Mordini (Riccardo), the commander of the firing squad, stepped forward towards the two ranks. He drew the squad to attention, turned to the condemned men and shouted: 'Prisoners, attention! About face!' Some raised their arms in the Fascist salute, others shouted 'Long live Italy,' and some looked bewildered and tried to say something. They all turned around slowly to face the lake except Francesco Barracu, who was at the end of the row and closest to Audisio and the Count; he stepped forward one pace and, pointing to the Gold Medal in the lapel of his jacket, said that he had the right to be shot in the chest. But the Colonel would have none of it and the old soldier stepped back in line without saying another word.

In the meantime, the platoon commander had stood his men at ease and turned the condemned men round again to stand opposite them. The minister Paolo Zerbino and the air force officer Pietro Calistri were allowed to coolly smoke a cigarette as a last request.

When the men were lined up again the order was barked: 'Prisoners, attention! About face!'

A great silence hung over the square.

'Squad, load!' 'Take aim!' One second more, then: 'Fire!'

A crackling volley of shots lasted only a few seconds. Then there was silence again while faint blue smoke from the guns rose gently into the air. The prior of the monastery, Father Santino Viale, stepped forward and gave a general benediction to the executed prisoners.

Suddenly, a voice in the crowd was heard to shout: 'Bring out Petacci!' Marcello Petacci was carried forward by two partisans, struggling violently, his face contorting with terror. He shouted: 'You can't shoot me, you mustn't. You're making a terrible mistake. After all that I've done for Italy. You can't.'

By now he had been taken as far as the row of corpses. Suddenly, with a powerful heave, he broke away from the men holding him and fled into the crowd, managing to force his way across the square and to run up a narrow street alongside the town hall.

He was only recaptured a hundred metres away, outside the Dongo Hotel where his partner, Zita Ritossa, and their two young boys were being held. Four men grabbed him and carried him bodily to the parapet. But he gave one last tremendous heave, shook himself free, jumped into the lake and began to swim out with powerful strokes. He did not get very far. A hail of bullets struck him and he suddenly stopped and disappeared slowly into the murky waters of the lake.

The bursts of shooting gradually died away. Valerio, who was still in great haste, sent for the furniture lorry that brought his men to Dongo and had the bodies loaded onto it. He told the Count to fish Petacci out of the lake and to have him buried in the local cemetery, which he refused to do, but sent some of his men in a boat to recover the corpse and place it on top of the others.

The lorry lumbered off for Milan, carrying away the bodies and the escort, followed by Audisio and Lampredi in their car. As the vehicles disappeared around the bend in the road, all they left behind was a great pool of blood at the foot of the parapet and a vague smell of gunpowder in the air.

When the lorry reached the junction at Azzano between the main road and the Via XXIV Maggio it stopped to pick up the bodies of Mussolini and Petacci that had been brought by car from the place of execution at Giulino. The vehicle with the eighteen bodies on board left for Milan and the journey went smoothly until it reached the city outskirts.

Outside the Pirelli factory in Via Fabio Filzi at ten in the evening the lorry was suddenly ordered to stop at a road block manned by royalist partisans of the Christian Democrat Ticino Division from Lake Maggiore. Valerio and his men were mistaken for Fascists owing to their brand new uniforms, lack of identity documents, and possession of papers from Mussolini's archive. The party was held at gunpoint and detained for four long hours until Lampredi was allowed to telephone the command of the military committee in Via Brera, who were able to vouch for them (in the process, also learning that the mission had been a total success).

At 3.40 a.m. the truck arrived in Piazzale Loreto, where Valerio ordered the unloading of the bodies on the ground exactly where the partisan victims of the slaughter of 10 August 1944 had been abandoned by Fascist soldiers, who had mocked them, left them exposed in the sun for the entire day, and prevented their families collecting their remains.

Valerio withdrew and left some of his men on guard. Within hours, the square began to be thronged with thousands of curious onlookers. At first the corpses rested on the concrete pavement, and Mussolini's head was laid mockingly in the lap of Petacci, while the mob vented their fury on the bodies.

At 11 a.m. a squad of firemen arrived in Piazzale Loreto with a tender and washed the bodies of blood, spit and vegetables, before hanging Mussolini, Petacci, and five others by the feet on the gantry of the petrol station on the corner between the square and the Corso Buenos Aires.

Around 1 p.m. a squad of partisans took the corpses down on the orders of the American troops who had just arrived in the city. Colonel Charles Poletti, incoming Allied Military Governor of Lombardy, described the spectacle as like something out of the Wild West, but, to the relief of some of the partisan leaders, did not criticise them over Mussolini's fate. Instead, he told them: 'We walked around Milan. We found order and discipline. We were very happy and express our satisfaction to the National Liberation Committee and the partisans for the work they have done.'

At a special meeting of the Liberation Committee in the Prefecture, Sandro Pertini said that it was necessary for them to issue an official communiqué stating that it had ordered the capture and shooting of Mussolini, so assuming responsibility for what happened. After a lively discussion, a resolution was adopted:

The CLNAI declares that the shooting of Mussolini and accomplices, which it ordered, is the necessary conclusion of an historical phase that leaves our country still covered with material and moral rubble and of an insurrectionary struggle that marks for the homeland the promise of rebirth and reconstruction. The Italian people could not begin a free and normal life - which Fascism denied them for twenty years - if the CLNAI had not promptly demonstrated its iron will to make their own a judgment already pronounced by history.

With the war ending, it seemed that everyone wanted to move on.

17 THE AMERICAN INVESTIGATION

The American military authorities were furious when they heard of the killing of Mussolini, Petacci, and the other leading Fascists, which flew both in the face of Allied policy and the desperate attempts of their own secret agents to capture them.

Instructions had been sent to all the Office of Strategic Services (OSS) operatives in the field 'to capture, protect, and bring back alive all important Fascist officials and German commanders, especially Mussolini, Graziani, and the members of Mussolini's puppet cabinet.' These orders were also sent to the leaders of the National Liberation Committee for general distribution among the partisan forces throughout German-occupied Italy.

The OSS immediately sent one of their leading secret agents to find out what had gone wrong. Forty-six-year-old Colonel Valerian Lada-Mocarski, agent 441, was chosen personally for the mission by Allen W. Dulles, head of OSS Switzerland and his former companion on the board of the J. Henry Schroder Banking Corporation in the United States. The Colonel had retired from the army, but was in Switzerland 'on a Government mission.'

He was born on 24 October 1898 in the legendary city of Samarkand in Turkestan, Russia, where his father was a Tsarist General. The family escaped the country after the 1917 revolution and the young man joined the French Army. On 15 December 1923, he embarked on the SS *Leviathan* at Cherbourg and landed in New York a week later. His naturalisation petition of 8 April 1925 showed him as a banker living at 14, Washington Square; he had married his American wife, Laura Klots, the previous year.

Lada-Mocarski joined the army with the rank of captain in 1940 and worked in the Lend-Lease Programme, but was soon recruited for OSS Secret Intelligence (SI) by Major-General William J. Donovan, Director of the OSS, going on to serve in the Middle East,

France, and finally Lugano, Switzerland. The accounts of the execution in Lada-Mocarski's two memorandums of May 1945, entitled *The Last Days of Mussolini and his Ministers*, confirm the time and place of the shooting as set out in the original article in the Communist newspaper, *Unità*.

According to the first report, written in early May, after the couple got out of the car in front of the Villa Belmonte, Mussolini was ordered to move a few paces towards the stone wall at the northern end of the gate. Almost simultaneously, Audisio's machine gun rang out. He was standing to the right of the dictator and his five shots hit him obliquely in the chest, bringing him to his knees before slumping sideways against the wall. It was then Petacci's turn. She lifted her arms in a desperate gesture, received several bullets in the chest and fell by the side of her lover, their bodies touching.

The second memorandum, dated 30 May, provided a different description of the mechanics of the execution. Now there was more than one killer and Valerio's personal weapon was a pistol and not a machine gun.

Following this account, the couple left the house in Bonzanigo at around 4 p.m. Mussolini wore a grey overcoat with the collar raised and a cap pulled down over his eyes; Claretta had a simple suit, with a silk scarf on her head; both wore black boots. The escort was led by Moretti, armed with a machine gun; followed by Lampredi, with a rifle on his shoulder; and, finally, by Audisio, with a revolver.

The dictator and his lover retraced their footsteps of the day before, climbing up the Via del Riale and then taking the Via Mainoni d'Intignano. Half way down that street, Mussolini suddenly seemed as if he were about to collapse, but recovered his composure straight away. The few passers-by they met were ordered to make themselves scarce, but some remained to observe the little procession.

Via Mainoni d'Intignano leads to a small square in which there was a long stone basin with constantly running water, the wash place of the village. On the eastern end of the square there is an arch at the start of Via XXIV Maggio, which winds down towards Azzano through Giulino. Audisio's car, a black Fiat 1100 with a Rome number plate, was parked under the arch. The party stopped here.

It was rather dark under the archway and the place would have lent itself to an execution. But the presence of two people nearby and another two by the wash basin led to a change of plan and prolonged the life of the couple by a few minutes. However, witnesses could not but notice the desperation with which Petacci hugged Mussolini during the brief stop.

They were then taken by car down the Via XXIV Maggio until it stopped opposite a gate bearing the number fourteen. At this point, the road bends suddenly, so that nothing is visible from the north, while the curved wall surrounding the gate also conceals the view from the south. Looking down and to the left towards the lake, one can make out a small peninsula and the trees of Tremezzo, with the hills around Bellagio as a backdrop. The view in front of the gate is hidden by a thick clump of trees. Beyond the gate, a short way up, stands the Villa Belmonte ('Beautiful Mountain').

In this beautiful place, Mussolini and Petacci were made to get out of the car. And it is probable that they now understood what was about to happen. Terrified and confused, they heard the sentence of death from Audisio. Mussolini was then ordered to move a few steps towards the wall, to the north of the gate. Shots were fired almost simultaneously from Audisio's revolver and from the machine gun of Moretti.

Audisio's two shots seemed to explode a fraction of a second before those fired from the machine gun of Moretti. The bullets of the revolver hit Mussolini obliquely on his back, while the three bullets fired by the machine gun hit him directly in the chest.

Moretti was positioned to the south of Mussolini, who fell on his side against the wall. Then it was the turn of Petacci. She raised her arms in a desperate gesture, was hit by several bullets in the chest and fell alongside her lover.

But Mussolini was not yet dead; one eye was still open and looking upwards. At that precise moment, Canali, an officer of the local partisan group, arrived from the road below, wanting to investigate the sound of gunfire. Lampredi recognised him and gestured him forward. Seeing that Mussolini was still alive, the new arrival finished him off with two shots of his pistol.

Afterwards, Canali was told by the partisan guard Giuseppe Frangi (Lino) that immediately before the execution Petacci asked Mussolini: 'Are you glad that I followed you to this bitter epilogue?' According to the partisan, it was a question which could have been inspired by love or by resentment.

The two partisan guards, Frangi and his companion, Guglielmo Cantoni (Sandrino), remained alongside the bodies, while their executioners left for Dongo.

Lada-Mocarski sent this second report to Allen Dulles in Switzerland on 30 May 1945, saying that thanks to eyewitnesses he had obtained enough material to cover the movements of Mussolini and his followers on 26, 27 and 28 April, as well as part of 25 April; he lacked a report of the meeting of Mussolini with Cardinal Schuster, but hoped to obtain one on his next visit to Milan in a day or two, based on direct testimonies. In this way, the last four days of the life of Mussolini would be covered.

Copies of the two secret memorandums were also forwarded to General Donovan and to Whitney Shepardson, who headed the Secret Intelligence branch of the OSS.

Following his assignment, Lada-Mocarski returned to the United States and resumed his employment with the J. Henry Schroder Banking Corporation, retiring as Vice-Chairman in 1964. His wife,

Laura, enjoyed bookbinding, while he collected rare books, particularly volumes on Alaska and travellers in old Russia.

In 1977, six years after Valerian had passed away, Laura gifted his collection of research notes, manuscript drafts, correspondence, photographs, and printed material on the events of 1945 to Yale University Library, catalogued as the 'Mussolini Collection of V. Lada-Mocarski.' [1]

The drafts are the basis of the two reports to the OSS in May 1945 and an article on his experiences in Italy for the renowned *Atlantic Monthly* magazine, published in December 1945 and headed 'The Last Three Days of Mussolini.' [2]

Strangely, Lada-Mocarski's account mirrored the 'official' or Communist version, which portrayed Colonel Valerio as the sole executioner of Mussolini and Petacci, completely ignoring the evidence of his own investigation.

1. Claretta Petacci reading Mussolini's book, *Storia di un Anno* (Story of a Year), published in 1944.

2. Benito Mussolini leaving the Prefecture in Milan, with SS bodyguard Fritz Birzer on his left, 25 April 1945.

3. The De Maria house in Bonzanigo, 1945. The room of Mussolini and Petacci was on the second floor of the right wing.

4. Walter Audisio (Colonel Valerio), 1963.

5. Michele Moretti (Pietro Gatti), c. 1942.

6. Count Pier Luigi Bellini delle Stelle (Pedro), 1944/1945.

7. Aldo Lampredi (Guido Conti), c. 1970.

8. Giuseppina Tuissi (Gianna), 1943.

9. Luigi Canali (Captain Neri), 1943.

10. Urbano Lazzaro (Bill) reconstructing the position of Mussolini's body after the shooting, October 1945.

11. Lazzaro indicating a bullet hole in the wall of the Villa Belmonte, October 1945.

12. The gate of the Villa Belmonte, with memorial cross to Mussolini on the left, 2011. Scene of pilgrimage for neo-fascists.

13. Mussolini's last journey. The purple line shows the route of his convoy; the red dotted lines indicate routes to Switzerland; and the yellow line shows the most direct route to the Valtellina.

18 THE EYEWITNESSES

Valerian Lada-Mocarski, American OSS agent 441, launched his enquiry into the executions by going to Como on the following day, Sunday, 29 April, and to Milan on Monday, the 30th. However, though only 24 hours had passed, he was not able to obtain authentic accounts in Como or even to locate any eyewitnesses there or in Milan.

Lada-Mocarski related: 'Without a doubt this was due to the fact that Mussolini was captured in a small town on the western shore of Lake Como and then shot on an isolated country road near Giulino di Mezzegra, on the hills that overlook the lake. Even the local population were kept well away from the events, and, with the exception of the protagonists in the drama, no one else witnessed the entire sequence of events.'

He added that there were only five people at the execution of Mussolini and Petacci. A few days later, one of these would be the victim of a fatal 'accident' and another would suffer a severe nervous breakdown before finally disappearing without trace.

Lada-Mocarski used cover names for most of the partisans in his reports, but the five eyewitnesses he was talking about were: Walter Audisio (Colonel Valerio), Aldo Lampredi (Guido Conti), Michele Moretti (Pietro Gatti), Giuseppe Frangi (Lino), and Luigi Canali (Captain Neri); it was Frangi who died and Canali who disappeared.

Lada-Mocarski visited all the places mentioned in his reports a few days after the incidents had taken place, including the De Maria house in which Mussolini and Petacci spent their last night.

This is how the agent described Bonzanigo: 'A small rural settlement in the hills a few kilometres from Azzano. The houses are dug into the rocks. The dark and tortuous roads bring to mind medieval intrigues and form the perfect setting for the dramatic events which have as its protagonist a despot of times gone by.'

Lada-Mocarski spoke to numerous people over the following month. On 9 May, he met General Raffaele Cadorna, the military leader of the partisans, who told him that not all the matters he was investigating were known to the members of the National Liberation Committee, adding that the practice was not to look too deeply into such matters. However, he confirmed that 'Colonel Valerio had been ordered to proceed with the execution at the time of his departure from Milan for Dongo.' In reply to the agent's question if this order was the result of a decision of the Committee and if he had been present when it was taken, Cadorna replied rather enigmatically: 'The order was officially enacted by a member of the Committee, who acted on behalf of the whole Committee.'

Gustavo Ribet, commander of the Justice and Liberty partisans for the region of Lombardy (in which Como is situated), also confirmed that the Committee did not assume responsibility for the execution until 24 hours after it had taken place. Lada-Mocarski noted that the official communication only appeared in the Milan press on Monday, 30 April, two days after the shootings.

In his first memorandum, the agent said that his description was based on a composite account provided by eyewitnesses and other people. They included Lia De Maria, who, together with her husband Giacomo, always spoke clearly of the three men arriving at their farmhouse at four in the afternoon and taking Mussolini and Petacci away. Another informant was Giuseppe Frangi (Lino), one of the two partisan guards, who was himself killed a few days later.

In a preface to the second memorandum, the agent noted that his description was based in part on the statements of eyewitnesses (once again including Lia De Maria) and in part on the written statements sent to him a few days later 'by the partisan officer who fired two shots as a coup de grace at Mussolini.' Though this informant is unnamed in the report, from the description of his part in the execution and of his subsequent disappearance, it is clear that he was talking about the 52nd Garibaldi Brigade's Chief of Staff, Luigi Canali, universally known as Captain Neri.

An account from another of the participants, Aldo Lampredi (Guido Conti), appeared when the *Unità* newspaper of 23 January 1996 published a secret and presumably unbiased report that he had compiled in 1972 at the request of Armando Cossutta, a leading Communist politician and a former partisan. It was then handed to the Secretary of the Italian Communist Party (the PCI) and finally held in the Gramsci Institute of Rome:

We went down on foot as far as the car and made the prisoners climb in. I sat alongside the driver, Audisio was on the rear fender, and perhaps Moretti was on the other one. The journey was short and soon we arrived at the gate of the Villa Belmonte where we had decided to proceed with the execution. While Audisio checked that there were no people around and perhaps waited for the arrival of 'Lino' and 'Sandrino' (who instead arrived after the shooting), I went to the door on the side where Mussolini was sitting, turned to him and said a few words to this effect: 'Who would have thought that you who so persecuted the Communists would have to settle scores with them?' Mussolini did not say anything; Petacci gave me a long questioning look, to which she must have found a cold response in my eyes.

Mussolini and Petacci were made to get out of the car and to go to the wall close to the gate. She was on the right of him. Audisio did not read any sentence, perhaps he said a few words, but I am not sure. He pointed his machine gun, but the weapon did not work. I was on his right and took the pistol that I had in the pocket of my overcoat and pressed the trigger, but to no effect: the pistol was jammed.

Then we called Moretti, who was on our left, towards the square with the wash house; Audisio took his machine gun and fired.

All this took place in the shortest time, one or two minutes, during which Mussolini remained motionless, dazed, while Petacci shouted that we must not shoot him and moved towards him almost as if she wanted to protect him with her body. It was perhaps the behaviour of the woman, so in contrast to his own, that led Mussolini at the last moment to jerk, straighten himself up, widen his eyes, and - opening the collar of his greatcoat - to exclaim: 'Aim at my heart.' These words seem more accurate than those reported by the driver Geninazza: 'Fire at my chest.'

The article confirmed Audisio's statement in his memoir that he fired at Mussolini and Petacci using the MAS submachine gun handed to him by Michele Moretti and that Lampredi had also tried to use his own pistol, which then misfired.

The driver, Giovanni Battista Geninazza, asserted that Audisio did not even go with Moretti and Lampredi to the De Maria house but remained with him in the square, limiting himself to firing a burst of machine gun fire like some sort of signal. However, he did confirm the transfer by car to the spot in front of the Villa Belmonte and also the jamming of the Colonel's submachine gun, recalling that he cursed and tore his pistol from its holster, but this also failed to fire. He then shouted 'Bring me your weapon' to Moretti, who ran back with his submachine gun. Mussolini unbuttoned his grey-green jacket, as if he was overcoming his fear for the first time, and said firmly 'Fire at my chest.' Claretta tried to grab the barrel while Audisio was shooting, but fell, hit in the heart.

Another version was provided to the journalist Ferruccio Lanfranchi by Guglielmo Cantoni (Sandrino), from Gera Lario, the surviving member of the two partisan guards in the De Maria house.

In the article entitled 'Sandrino Speaks,' which was published in the *Corriere d'Informazione* on 22-23 October 1945, he said that he had followed the party on foot, taking a short cut, and saw Valerio in front of the gate of Villa Belmonte fire a couple of pistol shots at Mussolini, who unexpectedly remained on his feet. At this point, Moretti intervened to mow down Mussolini and Petacci with a burst of submachine gun fire. Mussolini fell on one knee and one elbow; Petacci raised her arms, clenched her fists, and collapsed on him. Audisio also fired another two shots at Mussolini, who was still moving.

Both Cantoni and the journalist Ferruccio Lanfranchi were summoned to appear as witnesses at the 1957 trial in Padua on the so-called 'Gold of Dongo.' Cantoni said that he could not remember anything, retracted his previous statement, and claimed that he was not even present at the killing, while Lanfranchi confirmed point by point the account he had given him 12 years earlier.

The regional newspaper, the *Corriere Lombardo*, reported in 1956 that the partisans of the 52nd Brigade had always believed that it was Michele Moretti who was the prime mover in the death of Mussolini. According to their statements, after Audisio's submachine gun jammed, he killed Mussolini and then Petacci with two short bursts of gunfire. Audisio only fired the coup de grace at the dictator. [1]

After the war, Moretti briefly commanded a company of the semi-official 'People's Police' in Como, but migrated to Ljubljana in Yugoslavia in November 1945, remaining there until June of the following year after the issuing of an arrest warrant at the start of a case linked to the 'Gold of Dongo.' On returning to Italy, he remained in hiding until the cancellation of the warrant in May 1947 following the withdrawal of the accusations against him in the opening phase of proceedings. Moretti found employment as a factory worker in the Como area at the Pessina firm of silk processors and was appointed a union leader, but in 1954 was sacked after leading a strike, and then became a self-employed craftsman.

Moretti was an unassuming person and a loyal member of the Communist Party, which has always supported the 'official version' asserting that Walter Audisio was the executioner of the dictator. In the few interviews he gave, Moretti confirmed that the Colonel had shot Mussolini and Petacci with the MAS submachine he passed him; in 1973, he told author Candiano Falaschi that he also gave him a revolver, which was immediately returned to him afterwards.

Though the details may sometimes vary, the accounts clearly identify what some jurisdictions would nominate as several 'persons of interest' in the events surrounding the death of Mussolini and Petacci: Walter Audisio (Colonel Valerio), Luigi Canali (Captain Neri), Guglielmo Cantoni (Sandrino), Giuseppe Frangi (Lino), Aldo Lampredi (Guido Conti), and Michele Moretti (Pietro Gatti).

19 SUSPICIOUS DEATHS

Of the six partisan captors who drove Mussolini and Petacci towards Como and then back to Bonzanigo in the early hours on the last day of their lives, 28 April 1945, three would also die in the coming days: Luigi Canali (Captain Neri), Giuseppina Tuissi (Gianna), and Giuseppe Frangi (Lino). Only Count Pier Luigi Bellini delle Stelle (Pedro), Michele Moretti (Pietro Gatti), and Guglielmo Cantoni (Sandrino) survived.

There were also many other suspicious deaths among the ranks of former partisans - and sometimes also members of their families - in the Lake Como area. Most of the crimes were associated with the disappearance of the 'Gold of Dongo,' shorthand for all the valuables seized by the men of the 52nd Garibaldi Brigade from the Fascists in the convoy at the time of their capture.

On the evening of 28 April, a detailed inventory of the money and objects recovered from their luggage was made in the town hall in Dongo on the orders of Canali. The document was signed both by the brigade leaders: the Count, Moretti, Lazzaro, Canali, and Pietro Terzi (Francesco), who was the War Commissar, and by the women who counted the valuables: Giuseppina Tuissi (Gianna), Bianca Bosisio, and Teresa Moretti.

They found 1,357,000 Lire in banknotes, 72,000 Lire in cheques, 76,000 Swiss Francs, and 90 Pounds Sterling, but only a fountain pen, a medal, and a bracelet out of the many gold items that the prisoners had with them at the time of their capture.

Though two of the signatories of the inventory, the Count and Lazzaro, were royalists, a postscript was added that in view of the generous support of the local Communist Party during the partisan war, they would 'entrust' the valuables to the Como Federation. In a later court case, the Count said that this implied a temporary deposit, whereas Terzi claimed that it meant a permanent handover.

Luigi Canali disappeared nine days after the inventory was made. The cause may have lain with events earlier in the year. He had been captured together with his lover, Giuseppina Tuissi, during the night of 6 and 7 January at Villa di Lezzeno by the XI Black Brigade Cesare Rodini, and they were taken to the gaol of Como-Borghi and cruelly tortured. After three weeks, Tuissi gave her captors scraps of misleading information. She was then sent to the headquarters of the SS in Monza, but released on 12 March on the initiative of an officer of the Gestapo after being transferred to Rovereto and scheduled for deportation to a camp in Germany; this may have been out of pity, or in the hope that she would lead them to Canali, who had managed to escape from the jail on 29 January.

Senior Communists came to the conclusion that this was only possible with the collusion of the Fascists, particularly as Paolo Porta, the commander of the local Black Brigade, spread claims of his betrayal. Three weeks later, a so-called 'Tribunal of the People' was convened in the back room of Milanese grocery shop Spartaco in Piazzale Emilia to examine the couple's alleged treasonous behaviour on the orders of the General Command of the Garibaldi Brigades in Lombardy. Amerigo Clocchiatti (Ugo) presided and Pietro Vergani (Fabio) assumed the role of public prosecutor. The tribunal issued a sentence of death for the couple.

However, the Como partisans did not believe that they were traitors and had no intention of carrying out the sentence. After various adventures, the pair returned to their companions of the 52nd Brigade, who welcomed them back. Since the role of commandant had been given to the Count, Canali was appointed Chief of Staff, a role entirely unknown in other Garibaldi brigades.

On 29 April, Tuissi went to Como to hand over a wooden casket containing jewels from the inventoried items to Dante Gorreri at the Casa del Fascio, taken over as headquarters of the Communist Party Federation. She was subsequently arrested and held in the former

Generale Cantore barracks in Milan by members of the 113th Garibaldi Brigade to be investigated on the charges of betrayal. Tuissi was suddenly released on 9 May after being told by Vergani that Canali had been found guilty and executed by a partisan group in the mountains, adding that she was prohibited from going to Como.

On the evening of 6 May, the Captain had confided to his mother that he still had 'one mission to carry out.' The following morning he was picked up in a car by people he knew and taken to the prison of the 'People's Police' in the Villa Tornaghi (now demolished) at 33, Via Bellinzona, in the city centre; he was never seen again and his body was never found.

At the end of the month, Tuissi went with Alice, the sister of Canali, to meet Vergani in Milan in order to discover what he knew about the disappearance of her lover. The commander reacted angrily, saying: 'You are treating honest people as delinquents; you escaped once, you won't get a second chance.'

Reluctantly, Tuissi started her own investigation, despite the warnings and threats. She met Ferruccio Lanfranchi, editor of the *Corriere d'Informazione*, who was conducting his enquiry into the last days of Mussolini, and on 20 April she returned to Lake Como with Alice; among the people they interviewed were Pietro Terzi and Guglielmo Cantoni (Sandrino), one of the two former guards of Mussolini and Petacci at the De Maria house.

There are differing versions of what happened next, but what all the accounts have in common is that they say that Tuissi was seen in the company of two of her male comrades on the lakeside at Pizzo on the evening of 23 April. Then screams were heard, followed by gunshots and the departure of the two men. Tuissi was never seen or heard from again and her body was never recovered.

On the night of 4-5 May, the corpse of the other night-time guard of Mussolini and Petacci, Canali's friend Giuseppe Frangi, known as Lino, was discovered. On 5 July, the body of Anna Maria Bianchi, a friend and confidante of Tuissi, was found drowned after being tortured and wounded by two pistol shots. On the following night, Michele Bianchi, father of Anna Maria, was killed with two shots to the head.

After the war, public concern and a journalistic campaign led to growing demands for justice. In October 1949, twenty people, including former partisans, members of the Communist Party, and citizens of Dongo and the surrounding area were sent for trial at the Appeals Court of Milan on charges including aggravated murder, embezzlement, theft, and receiving stolen goods.

According to a report by the Dongo police prepared as part of the evidence, Frangi had been assassinated with a burst of machine gun fire at point-blank range by an unknown person, perhaps one of his own men; earlier accounts had suggested that he was killed in a banal incident, mishandling his weapon after returning from a trip on the lake by boat.

The proceedings were planned to be brief, but new evidence and legal problems led to long delays. On 29 April 1957, the trial on the disappearance of the 'Gold of Dongo' and the mysterious chain of associated crimes opened in the Assize Court of Padua, presided over by Doctor Augusto Zen. Thirty-six people, indicted by separate orders of 3 October 1949 and 12 November 1952, were accused of crimes against life, personal safety, and property.

Among the defendants was Dante Gorreri for having taken delivery of the 'Gold of Dongo' and being responsible for its disappearance. With Pietro Vergani he was also accused of having arranged the killing of Tuissi and Anna Maria Bianchi. In addition, Vergani was accused of ordering the killing of Canali, for reasons of hate and vengeance and his perceived insubordination. Also accused of the killing of Tuissi was Maurizio Bernasconi (Mirko); Dionisio Gambaruto for that of Canali; and Natale Negri and Ennio Pasquali

(Nado) for that of Anna Maria Bianchi. It proved impossible to charge anyone for the murder of her father, Michele.

Gorreri (Guglielmo), the wartime local Communist leader, and Vergani (Fabio), the Communist partisan commander, were both well-known personalities and successful parliamentarians in the ranks of the party after the war.

Gorreri was born in Parma on 15 May 1900. A plumber by trade, he was sentenced to a total of ten years imprisonment as a Communist agitator, which he served in three different island prisons. In 1942, Gorreri returned home to organise the underground Communist Federation and following the Armistice of September 1943 helped organise the local partisan movement. In May 1944, he was sent to carry out the same role in Como. Gorreri was captured by troops of the Black Brigades on 21 January 1945, but was allowed to escape on 1 February by the detachment leader. He re-emerged in Como on 28 April as Secretary of the Communist Federation and soon took over the Casa del Fascio for the Communist Party and began exacting retribution on alleged collaborators.

Pietro Vergani was born on 14 October 1907 in Cinisello Balsamo, near Milan. He was a union organiser and Communist from a young age, attending the 4th Congress in Cologne in 1931 and later the Leninist University in Moscow. He returned to organise the party's underground activity in Liguria, but was arrested in 1933 and sentenced to seven years and six months imprisonment by a special tribunal. Freed in 1941, Vergani resumed his clandestine activity, but following the re-emergence of Mussolini as head of the Social Republic, was rearrested by Fascist police in October 1943. Freed again in January 1944, Vergani went on to become inspector of the Garibaldi Brigades in Lombardy, commander of the local military committee, and finally a vice-commandant in Milan.

At the end of the war, he was awarded the Italian Silver Medal for Military Valour.

Walter Audisio, who had long since admitted to being 'Colonel Valerio,' author of the shooting of Mussolini, Petacci, and their leading followers, was not among the accused at the Padua trial, but appeared as a witness. Also a parliamentary deputy belonging to the Communist party, he had already been investigated in other proceedings (and would be again), but was never found guilty.

Another of the witnesses, Enrico Mattei, former administrative officer for the military committee, stated that 'the spoils of acts of war belong to the formations that captured them, and could be put at the disposition of the commanders.' Another influential witness, Luigi Longo, said: 'I do not believe that any valuables went to the Communist Party. Instead, they were given to a *Garibaldino* command that was authorised to dispose of any spoils of war to its detachments.'

Intriguingly, one payment is said to have been made to the accountant Walter Audisio for the trip on 28 April, signed off as: 'Reimbursement of expenses to Colonel Valerio for mission to Dongo: four thousand Lire.' [1]

There were forty-four hearings at the trial, which saw the appearance of fifty lawyers and three hundred witnesses over almost three months. But on 24 July one of the auxiliary judges, nobleman and First World War veteran, Silvio Andrighetti, was hospitalised, and proceedings were suspended. He committed suicide at home on 13 August and the trial was postponed once again.

It was never resumed and the enactment of amnesties in the early 1970s ended any chance of further legal proceedings concerning the disappearance of the 'Gold of Dongo' or its associated crimes. This also marked the end of the possibility of any detailed and systematic look at the last hours of Mussolini and Petacci by the Italian State.

20 OSS AGENTS ~ 1

From early April 1945, all field operatives of the United States Office of Strategic Services (OSS) were under orders 'to capture, protect, and bring back alive all important Fascist officials and German commanders, especially Mussolini, Graziani, and the members of Mussolini's puppet cabinet.'

In addition, the instructions were sent to the leaders of the National Liberation Committee for general distribution among the partisan forces throughout German-occupied Italy.

The OSS was also able to mobilise agents from its covert base across the border in Lugano, Switzerland.

They launched their first mission on 26 April 1945 'to ensure that Mussolini and his followers were consigned into the hands of the authorities as soon as possible' and 'to obtain the demobilisation and disarmament of the Fascist forces gathering in Como.'

Directing affairs was the American Vice-Consul in Lugano, Donald Pryce Jones, agent 809. Both friends and enemies knew that the Consulate, housed in a secluded villa in the Paradiso suburb, was cover for the OSS and that former newspaper reporter Jones was Allen Dulles's man in the Italian-speaking canton of Ticino in southern Switzerland.

Dulles wrote that he was 'deeply involved with their operations with the Italian anti-Fascist partisan elements in the border area and was well known to them as 'Scotti.'

The duties of Jones were to observe developments in Italy, collect intelligence, coordinate agents, provide communications and finances, maintain good relations with Swiss military intelligence and police, and, where possible, neutralise the activity of enemy secret services.

The men given the new OSS mission were both Italians: Captain Giovanni Dessy and Doctor Salvatore Guastoni. The youngest of the pair, frigate captain Dessy, had taken part in an Allied mission codenamed Nemo, described in the official records as: 'Perhaps the most efficient and comprehensive espionage network in northern Italy.' The doctor, once a Fascist, was a law graduate, stockbroker, and army veteran, and from 1944 had worked with the OSS and the intelligence service of the Italian Royal Navy.

It was Guastoni, who knew the Como area well, who crossed the threshold of the Lugano Consulate to see Donald Jones on 26 April, as many other anti-fascists from Italy did in those days.

Jones, whom the partisans had also nicknamed their 'American uncle,' was not very tall, portly, and kindly. He listened carefully as Guastoni told him that if he and Dessy were given written authorisation to act on behalf of the Consulate, they would try and obtain the surrender of the Fascist forces making for Como.

Jones agreed enthusiastically and had the document prepared. It read:

The Foreign Service of the United States, Department of State, Consulate-General Lugano: Doctor Salvatore Guastoni, in our service and that of the Italian Navy, is authorised to negotiate the transfer of power in the best way possible, avoiding any casualties.

Signed: Donald Jones, Lugano 26 April 1945

In Como, the Liberation Committee of six people from the major political parties had held a clandestine meeting the day before to discuss the situation. Members heard a report from lawyer Lorenzo Spallino of the Christian Democrats regarding talks he held with Renato Celio, the Fascist Prefect of Como and head of the province. Aware of the imminent collapse of the regime, he wanted to meet the Committee to discuss a transition towards a new government.

Armed with the authorisation from Jones, Guastoni and Dessy

arrived in Como and found that Celio was already negotiating with members of the Liberation Committee over the evacuation of Fascist forces and had also sent a message to the Vice-Consul to explore the possibility of Mussolini surrendering to the Americans.

Celio assured the agents that power would be handed over to the Resistance as soon as possible and suggested that the dictator's surrender could be obtained if his safety and that of his family was guaranteed.

When the Prefect also mentioned that he had the possibility of seeing Mussolini or of sending someone to meet him, Guastoni visited Jones again to establish the point of view of the Allies. He said that it was not possible to guarantee the lives of the dictator and his followers, as they would be subject to due legal process, but that those of the members of his family would be spared.

At the same time, the situation on the ground deteriorated, as Fascist forces had been told by radio to head for Como and were already arriving in large numbers across the province. The two agents passed on Jones's instructions for the surrender to Celio, who in turn told Alessandro Pavolini, founder and commander of the Black Brigades, who had entered Como on the morning of 26 April with the Milan detachment of about 1,500 men, seven armoured cars, and a hundred vehicles.

In order to avoid armed conflict, the Prefect went ahead with his meeting with members of the Liberation Committee and the partisan command in the Prefecture. They were very suspicious, but, with the aid of Doctor Guastoni and Captain Dessy as mediators, agreement was reached that the Fascists would cease military operations and start leaving the city for a demobilisation point at 6 a.m. on the 27th; in that period, no partisan activity would be mounted against them and the Committee would be able to assume control of the city.

The transfer went smoothly, there were no acts of violence, and Celio was placed under house arrest in his own apartment in the

Prefecture. Captain Dessy coordinated the surrender of the troops, trucks, and weapons in the grounds of the neo-classical Villa Olmo. Meanwhile, a small breakaway column consisting of Pino Romualdi, Vice-Secretary of the Fascist Republican Party; Colonel Francesco Colombo, leader of the notorious Autonomous Mobile Legion Ettore Muti; and Stefano Motta, commander of the XIII Black Brigade Marcello Turchetti, was rounded up by partisans at Cernobbio and returned to Como.

The first public meeting of the Liberation Committee was held in order to nominate a Socialist lawyer, Virginio Bertinelli, as the new Prefect. Captain Dessy told the members that he and Doctor Guastoni hoped to convince Mussolini to surrender to the Americans. The Committee issued the Captain with a document, which granted him: 'The widest and most absolute powers in negotiations of any kind with any person, military or otherwise, to carry out a mandate of special importance for the nation.' The pass was signed by the military commander, Major Cosimo Maria De Angelis, and counter-signed by the new Prefect, Virginio Bertinelli.

An opening for the mission had already appeared on the evening of 26 April when Vittorio Mussolini, eldest son of the dictator, asked Celio to organise a meeting with Doctor Guastoni with the object of reaching an agreement for the surrender of his father. It was decided that an urgent mission would be sent to the area where it was thought that he had found shelter and to ask him in the name of his family to surrender unconditionally to the authorities, so putting an end to all resistance on Italian territory.

Captain Dessy set out in a car at around 12.30 on 27 April, taking with him Pino Romualdi, Francesco Colombo, and Giovanni Teodorani, Mussolini's nephew, to represent the family. However, they were stopped at a roadblock in Cadenabbia by a group of partisans belonging to the Justice and Liberty movement. One of them recognised Colombo and an angry crowd soon gathered, putting the whole party at risk of being killed. The rebel commander, 'Giovanni,' ordered the arrest of the occupants of the car and had them locked in a nearby prison and then taken by lorry to San Fedele d'Intelvi. 'Giovanni' telephoned Como and when the mission's authenticity was confirmed its members were allowed to return, apart from Colombo; he was put against a wall and shot at Lenno next day at a spot where four partisans had been executed on 3 October 1944.

Captain Dessy hoped to resume the search for Mussolini on a second day, but at 10.30 in the evening received the official news that the dictator and the other Fascist leaders had been arrested at around 4 p.m. in Dongo.

Meanwhile, another marauding Fascist convoy was threatening Como. A column of three thousand troops of the Black Brigades, well-armed with canons and machine guns, had advanced from Lecco in two hundred trucks and halted on the outskirts of the city. The men had travelled for two days, suffering casualties in clashes with partisans, and had been told that they would only find food and shelter once they occupied the city. In view of their superiority in numbers, the decision was taken by the partisans to seek to prevent this at all costs and if possible to disarm them.

After a meeting between Guastoni and members of the Liberation Committee on the one hand, and the ex-prefect Celio and the Black Brigades' commander, Gino Gallarini, on the other, by late evening it was agreed that the troops could enter the city one vehicle at a time and under escort as far as the Fascist headquarters, where they would hand over their weapons and be allowed to go home. The surrender operations were carried out by late morning of the 28th without incident.

In his official report, Captain Dessy also wrote about the other major event of that day:

In the early hours, 'Colonel Valerio' of the General Military Command of Milan and *Signor* Guido, who introduced himself as a member of the same General Command, arrived at the Prefecture with the task of taking the arrested men back to Milan.

The Colonel was accompanied by an armed escort composed of about ten men. The National Liberation Committee provided the means of transport requested by 'Valerio' (a lorry completely covered with a tarpaulin) and assigned me and one of his men to guard the vehicle. Before leaving, 'Colonel Valerio' said, in a way that did not allow discussion, that he only wanted to have with him the representative of the National Liberation Committee [Oscar Sforni] and the provincial commandant, Major De Angelis. Therefore, the expedition left without me.

The rest is history. Concluding his report, Captain Dessy wrote: 'All the negotiations of a military character conducted by us during the days 26, 27, and 28 April were endorsed by Colonel Sardagna (belonging to the General Command and sent by General Cadorna), who arrived in Como on the morning of 27 April.'[1]

The Italian OSS agents' mission was effectively over. They had not captured Mussolini or his followers, but by negotiating the surrender of the large number of Fascist troops in the Como area had prevented the deployment of the only force that could have saved their lives.

21 OSS AGENTS ~ 2

In the story of Mussolini's final days the inaction of the German Army in defending him reflected a new reality that brought friend and foe together in a desperate search for self-survival and the end of the war.

After authorising the Guastoni-Dessy mission on 26 April, OSS agent Donald Jones went into the front line himself in an attempt to save Karl Wolff, SS-*Obergruppenführer* and General of the Military SS, Highest SS and Police Leader, Military Plenipotentiary of the German Armed Forces in Italy, Commander of the Rear Military Area and the Military Administration, and Himmler's personal representative.

Unknown to the outside world, since the end of February 1945 messages and envoys had been passing between the OSS mission in Switzerland and a group of German generals in Italy, with the aim of ending the conflict.

Wolff was the leader of the dissident officers and on the evening of 25 April had taken a train back into Italy after finalising the details of a secret surrender with Allen Dulles in Switzerland (an operation known to history as Sunrise).

The head of Swiss Military Intelligence for the Ticino Canton then telephoned Jones with the news that the General had now been completely surrounded by partisans at the SS command post in Cernobbio, the requisitioned Villa Locatelli, and that there was the danger that they might storm it and kill him and all the other officers inside.

Dulles decided on a rescue mission and sent two of his best helpers, Captain Max Waibel of Swiss Military Intelligence and Gero von Schulze Gaevernitz, a German-born naturalised American Citizen, to the Italian border crossing at Chiasso. When the pair alighted from the train they were surprised to be met by Jones and

OSS Captain Emilio Daddario. 'I understand that you want to liberate General Wolff,' said Jones. By ten o'clock that evening, he had organised the expedition, though Daddario was persuaded not to go along too. As Dulles recalled: 'Things were touchy enough without having an American army officer liberating an SS general. At least Scotti was a civilian.'

To the astonishment of the would-be rescuers, the partisans had neglected to cut the telephone wires to the Villa Locatelli. General Wolff was contacted and told that a convoy was shortly going to try to get through to him and that he was to make sure that they would not be shot at when they arrived.

The party crossed the border into Italy in three cars and disappeared into the darkness. The first carried two German SS officers from the dissolved border post and was decorated with white flags; Jones and three local Swiss followed in the second; and armed partisans brought up the rear in the third.

Almost as soon as they got under way, the men were greeted with rifle fire from rebels. Jones jumped out of his car and stood in the headlights, hoping that they would recognise him and stop firing. The partisan commander rushed out of the gloom and flung his arms around *lo zio americano* ('the American uncle') and the danger was over. The convoy soon reached Como, where the Resistance was taking over, and they were issued with the necessary papers to pass through partisan roadblocks.

After minor misadventures, including more rifle fire and the occasional lobbed hand grenade, the party reached Cernobbio and was safely guided past the guards by the two German officers in the lead car. Wolff was waiting in full SS uniform, which would not have gone down at all well with the partisans, so he was told to hurry and put on civilian clothes. The General offered his saviours Scotch whisky and some Lucky Strike cigarettes, which he said Rommel had captured in North Africa.

Every partisan group the rescuers met on the return journey led to fresh negotiations, arguments, and the checking of papers. Wolff was kept out of sight in the back of Jones's car and, strangely, the rebels never checked any of the vehicles.

The little convoy wound its way safely back to the Chiasso frontier post, arriving at around 2.30 on the morning of 27 April. They were welcomed by Waibel and Von Schulze Gaevernitz, who drove the General to a small hotel in Lugano. While waiting for the dawn, he told them of the events of the previous 24 hours.

He had been in continuous telephone communication with the SS commander in Milan, Colonel Walter Rauff, who was barricaded with his men in their headquarters at the Albergo Regina. The Colonel was the General's contact with Cardinal Ildefonso Schuster, to whom both Germans and Italians had turned in the search of a peaceful outcome to the conflict. Rauff reported that there was a stand-off between Germans and partisans in the centre of Milan, which threatened to destroy the chances of any peace agreement. The General ordered him to avoid clashes with the rebels at all costs and to release all political prisoners.

Rauff had tried to send an armoured car to pick up Wolff, but it could not break through the partisan roadblocks. Cardinal Schuster was also told of the General's predicament and sent a car towards Cernobbio with a priest and an SS officer on board, but they too had to turn back.

Wolff had received an unexpected visitor at Cernobbio in the shape of Marshal Rodolfo Graziani, the Fascist Minister of National Defence and commander of Army Group Liguria. After leaving Mussolini's convoy and consulting with his subordinates near Como he heard that General Wolff was in the area at the Villa Locatelli and rushed to see him on the morning of 26 April. During the course of their discussions, Graziani handed over a document that gave Wolff the power to surrender the Italian Fascist forces alongside the

Germans. Mussolini, who was moving north in his convoy, was not consulted or even aware of Graziani's move. As we shall see, the Marshal would surrender to OSS agent Captain Daddario shortly afterwards.

When Wolff was safely in Switzerland he noted at the bottom of the Marshal's document: 'I hereby delegate the above authorisation to my Chief Adjutant, Major [Eugen] Wenner.' This officer went on to sign the secret surrender to the Allies on the General's behalf at Caserta on 29 April, with Lieutenant-Colonel Victor von Schweinitz signing for Lieutenant-General Heinrich von Vietinghoff-Scheel, Commander-in-Chief South-West and Army Group C, and Lieutenant-General William Duthie Morgan signing on behalf of Field Marshal the Honourable Sir Harold Alexander.

The official secret history of SOE noted that 'the German High Command had by this time moved far from the Wagnerian vision of North Italy in flames and a last stand in the German Alps: resistance was now relevant only to the timing of surrender and the preservation of military honour.' [1]

In this atmosphere, it is easy to see how Mussolini's theoretical German allies were unwilling to lift a finger to save his life when he needed help most.

22 OSS AGENTS ~ 3

On 26 April 1945, another leading member of the Office of Strategic Services crossed the Swiss border, carrying orders to capture Mussolini and to become the American Liaison Officer with the National Liberation Committee in Milan.

Emilio Quincy Daddario, known to his friends as Mim, was born to Italian parents of Abruzzo origin in Massachusetts on 24 September 1918. A noted athlete in his youth, after graduating from the Wesleyan University in Middletown and the Connecticut University School of Law, he opened his own legal practice.

Recruited as OSS agent 774, Daddario arrived at the base in Palermo just in time to join the convoy to a new headquarters in Brindisi at the end of December 1943, where he became the Assistant Operations Officer to agent Max Corvo. Over the coming year he also often acted as temporary station head while Corvo travelled between various OSS and Army headquarters (later describing Daddario as his closest collaborator, who was acquainted with all the missions and personnel operating behind enemy lines).

Born in Augusta, Sicily, on 29 May 1920, Corvo had arrived in the United States with his mother and two siblings at the age of nine to be reunited with his father, Cesare, who had gone there following Fascist persecution. Max volunteered for the Army in 1941 and at Fort Lee, Virginia, drew up a plan for the development of partisan warfare in the Mediterranean Theatre. It so impressed senior officers that he was speedily transferred to the OSS, going on to become the Operations Officer of the Secret Intelligence branch in Italy.

As 1944 was drawing to a close, Corvo decided to send Daddario to Lugano to represent OSS Italy and to ensure proper communication with Allen Dulles and Donald Jones, who were also running operations into the north of the country, which was causing some administrative problems. Daddario arrived in Switzerland on

19 February 1945. By this time, twenty-nine of their missions were operating north of the Gothic Line, with radio links established with the Allied High Command, the Liberation Committee in Milan, and the individual partisan formations.

On the same day, Corvo closed down their Brindisi base, while Siena, a forward base since July 1944, became the final operational headquarters for OSS Secret Intelligence until the end of the war.

He recalled that in early April 1945 he sent instructions by radio and courier to Daddario (by now promoted from lieutenant to captain) to cross the Swiss frontier once the rising of the partisan forces got underway.

He was to move to Milan to take Mussolini as a prisoner of war, set up a headquarters, and establish liaison with General Cadorna and the Liberation Committee as the official Army and OSS representative. Another agent, Lieutenant Aldo Icardi, was also ordered to move with Cino Moscatelli's Valsesia partisan division to join forces with Daddario.

To coordinate the OSS personnel on the German collapse and render immediate assistance to the partisans, Corvo planned to parachute into the San Siro racetrack, near the centre of Milan, together with some of the younger members of the city team. A cablegram was sent from Allied Force Headquarters to the military committee on the afternoon of 27 April: 'Major Corvo and two men will be dropped on the San Siro hippodrome tomorrow morning, Saturday. Prepare reception and confirm urgently.'

However, at the last minute the plan was cancelled by the Allied headquarters in Caserta for security reasons and Corvo was told to proceed overland. Once he had sent the signal to Daddario at Lugano to move south to Milan, he left Siena at the head of an armed convoy to try and get there himself as soon as possible. They stopped briefly at OSS headquarters (Company D) in Florence to contact the Secret Intelligence mission leaders who were moving with the partisans. Corvo instructed Captain Arthur Latina to transmit all priority messages to their field radio, which would keep them in touch with headquarters during the journey to Milan; once there, they would set up a regular communication schedule.

Corvo recalled that on 26 April he received news that Daddario had crossed the Swiss frontier into Italy with a small armed group and was heading for Como. He had no way of contacting him until he reached Milan, but expectations were high:

Having completely briefed him on the objectives of his mission, we knew that unless something unforeseen happened he would carry out his important assignments, chief among which was the capture of Mussolini. [1]

Daddario's party moved steadily southwards along the narrow road alongside Lake Como until they met an open beige-coloured car south of Menaggio that was going in the opposite direction. A heavily-armed man leapt out and introduced himself as Lieutenant Vittorio Bonetti, a partisan commander and veteran of the war in Libya. He was amazed to see his first American soldier in Lombardy, recalling that Daddario had classic features, with short, black, curly hair, and an athletic build, which was enhanced by his uniform and a khaki forage cap on his head.

Bonetti told him that the partisans had surrounded the headquarters of the SS in the Villa Locatelli at Cernobbio and that the occupants included Marshal Rodolfo Graziani, Minister of National Defence for the RSI and commander of Army Group Liguria, as well as generals Ruggero Bonomi and Rosario Sorrentino. At 5.15 in the afternoon the partisans had given the occupants of the villa an ultimatum to surrender within 30 minutes or face attack.

Daddario decided to take the senior Fascist officers away from the villa with him to prevent needless loss of life when there was no further need for combat. Another passenger in the partisans' car, a lawyer representing the Como National Liberation Committee called Orsenigo, was thanked for his cooperation and requested to stop all partisan action so that a ceasefire could be agreed with the SS.

Daddario approached the villa together with Bonetti under a white flag and was admitted after saying that he was an American officer. The German troops were at their posts and the commanding officer, Captain Joseph Voetterl, said that he had orders not to surrender to the partisans. However, after a long discussion it was agreed that his troops would remain segregated until the arrival of Allied forces, when they would be completely disarmed; in the meantime, Daddario agreed that a quarter of their weapons could be retained, as he could not guarantee them protection from partisan attack.

Daddario was also worried about the safety of his Fascist prisoners and asked Bonetti to obtain transport for them. He requisitioned several vehicles, including the Marshal's staff car, so that a convoy of five was able to leave Cernobbio with about ten armed men. Graziani was in the lead car with Daddario and Bonetti, while Bonomi and Sorrentino travelled in other vehicles. The party managed to pass through numerous road blocks on the way to Como by stating: 'Special mission of the Allied High Command.'

Daddario met the Liberation Committee in the city and told them that he was going to see the commander of the German garrison, General Hans Leyers, with the hope of moving all his troops into the stadium until the arrival of Allied forces. The General agreed and said that three quarters of their arms would be immediately put into trucks for delivery to the Allied troops, while they would retain one quarter for personal protection; meanwhile, partisan guards patrolled at some distance to prevent any undue incident.

Daddario obtained a pass from the new prefect, Virginio Bertinelli, which asked all local military committees to give priority to the American mission on their journey to General Cadorna's headquarters in Milan. As the Captain was not able to be present when the Allies arrived, he left fellow OSS agent Larry Bigelow to explain the situation to the first American forces that reached the city, and he learnt later that everything went as planned.

With the convoy now composed of six vehicles the party headed for Milan at about 11 p.m. on 26 April. All roadblocks were negotiated without incident, but when they entered the city they were immediately attacked by unknown elements with automatic fire; no men were lost, but three cars were put out of action and the other three were damaged.

Daddario ordered that they should be drawn up in a secluded place and the men placed in strategic places to await daybreak. However, they were suddenly challenged by a German soldier. Daddario replied that he would like to speak to the man's commanding officer, figuring that they were in a talking rather than a fighting mood. He was told to wait for a reply and shortly afterwards was led to the SS headquarters in the Albergo Regina to meet Colonel Walter Rauff, commander of the SS and police.

The German troops were barricaded in several buildings in Milan, where they had orders to resist all partisan activity and only surrender to Allied troops. Bonetti recalled that Daddario, after introducing himself and not acknowledging Rauff's salute, asked him to shelter the prisoners for the night and to provide him with a telephone link to General Cadorna; he finished with the words: 'That is an order, Colonel!'

Daddario promised to do everything to maintain the status quo as long as the Germans surrendered immediately on the arrival of Allied forces. However, Rauff said that he had orders to fight and would follow them until he heard from General Wolff, who had gone to Switzerland to meet Allen Dulles. Since he had received no word and the General had said that he would return to Italy immediately, he felt that he could not act. In the circumstances, it was agreed that Daddario would return next day for further discussions.

The Captain then paid a visit to the partisan headquarters in Via Brera to discuss the whole situation with General Cadorna. The unexpected arrival of this American captain in the middle of the night caused consternation among many of the rebel leaders.

The General agreed that everything possible should be done to prevent fighting in the city and also said that he would accompany Daddario when he met Rauff again, but added that the only terms would be immediate surrender to the partisans.

During his encounter with Cadorna, Daddario asked: 'What is the latest information on Mussolini?'

'To date we have no information whatsoever,' the General replied.

Ironically, Daddario's presence allowed partisan scheming to ratchet up another notch, as Max Corvo recalled:

On 27 April, Daddario was already in Milan and had established contact with General Cadorna. When Walter Audisio was sent on the special mission to pick up Mussolini he used an identification document that was signed by Daddario to facilitate his mission. Since Daddario was the Allied officer officially accredited to CLNAI, he had been asked to sign numerous documents of this type. He was not aware, however, that Audisio had received orders to execute Mussolini or that Lampredi, who was vice-chief of the Communist Garibaldi Brigade, was going along with him. The National Liberation Committee had been told that Mussolini was to be captured alive and turned over to be tried by a high Allied Tribunal.[2]

The document read:

Milan, 28 April 1945. Colonel Valerio (otherwise known as Magnoli, Giovan Battista di Cesare) is an Italian officer belonging to the General Command of the Volunteers of Liberty. He is sent on a mission by the National Liberation Committee for northern Italy to Como and its province and must therefore be allowed to circulate freely with his armed escort.

The conference at the Albergo Regina was held in the afternoon and it was also attended by General Heinz Wening, commander of the *Wehrmacht* troops in Milan. It was finally agreed that he and Rauff would attempt to neutralise German forces converging on the city and ensure that their men remained at their posts until Allied troops arrived, at which time they would surrender. The agreement had the support of the Liberation Committee and was strictly adhered to even when Cino Moscatelli arrived at the head of 1,500 Communist partisans with the intention of attacking the Germans.

A senior American officer, Colonel John Fisk, also arrived at the Grand Hotel in the afternoon as the representative of General Willis Crittenberger, commander of 4th Corps. After hearing of the situation in the city from Daddario, he accepted the surrender of all SS troops from Colonel Rauff and then went on to Piazza Brescia, where General Wening surrendered the *Wehrmacht* troops.

Marshal Graziani and generals Bonomi and Sorrentino had been transferred the short distance from the Albergo Regina to the temporary headquarters of the American Mission at the Grand Hotel et de Milan in Via Manzoni (once home to the composer Giuseppe Verdi). The partisans had formed a cordon and held back a menacing crowd, but when the bodies of Mussolini and the other Fascist leaders arrived in the city on 29 April, the cry arose for Graziani to share their fate. Even the guards from the Socialist Party gave Daddario an ultimatum to immediately turn the Marshal over to the Liberation Committee.

In the end, together with fellow OSS agent Aldo Icardi, who had arrived in the city the day before, Daddario had to race up the stairs and stand in front of the door to the Marshal's room to prevent him being taken away. The partisans backed down and left them with a flood of oaths.

Daddario went to see General Cadorna and he agreed that the captives could be moved to the San Vittore jail. The transfer itself went smoothly, but an explosion took place in the car assigned to the Marshal and as a result Lieutenant Bonetti was badly wounded, losing the sight in one eye.

Colonel Fisk had orders to evacuate the prisoners and when Daddario again called on Cadorna for assistance he explained that he had been attending a meeting to form a tribunal to judge Graziani. However, he agreed that this was irregular and said that the Captain could take the trio out of San Vittore as long as it was done immediately. Daddario went to the jail with a car and three jeeps that Fisk had brought as an escort and drove towards the motorway. Several miles outside Milan the prisoners were transferred to the vehicles and delivered safely to the headquarters of the United States 4th Corps, then situated near Bergamo.

In a cablegram to Corvo on 29 April, Daddario reported that Mussolini and other Fascist leaders had been shot at Giuliano di Mezzegra, near Como, 'after a summary process.' Corvo had left Bologna with his armed convoy earlier that day and driven northwards along the Via Emilia until arriving at the Grand Hotel in the evening.

On the afternoon of 30 April, Daddario and Cadorna met General Crittenberger on the outskirts of Milan and he thanked them both for the conditions which Colonel Fisk found in the city. It was on this day that American troops arrived in force for the first time.

Daddario was left to close OSS Secret Intelligence operations in the city, until both he and Icardi were repatriated via Casablanca at the end of August 1945. They were awarded the Italian Silver Medal for Military Valour on the personal recommendation of General Cadorna, as well as the United States Legion of Merit.

Marshal Graziani had constantly talked of doing something for Daddario and Icardi to show his gratitude to them for saving him from the partisans, and before he left them he said: 'Take Embaye, and treat him well, he will be a good servant.' The young man was an Ethiopian prince who had been given to the Marshal as a gift by a favour-seeking chief while he was in East Africa. Embaye spoke Italian and English and was taken over by the OSS agents, acting as their butler until they finally left Italy for the United States. They also raided the motor pool at the Albergo Regina and selected a beautiful Lancia sports car, which served them handsomely during the vacation days that followed the end of war.

On 15 June 1945, Marshal Graziani had written to Daddario from a prison camp in Algeria: 'I would like to thank you most profoundly from my heart for what you did for me in those very dangerous times. There is no doubt that I owe you my salvation during the days of 26, 27, and 28 April. For this my heart is full of gratitude and I will never forget it as long as I live.' At the end of the letter the Marshal added a request: 'I beg you to write to me to confirm that the item I left you reached its destination.'

In a second message of 29 April 1945, Daddario had told Corvo that after an agreement with the Liberation Committee he had interned Graziani, Bonomi, and Sorrentino in the San Vittore jail and that he was 'in possession of their personal papers.'

In the peaceful days after the war, when the pair often met, Corvo asked point blank: 'Eh, Mim, what finally became of Graziani's secret diary?' The reply was only a shrug and a long silence.

23 SOE AGENTS ~ 1

What was the role of the Special Operations Executive during the last days of Mussolini? By April 1945, they had over two hundred men in the field, made up of 59 British officers, 66 'other ranks,' and 92 Italian agents.

The secret agency also had a senior agent acting as Liaison Officer with the National Liberation Committee in Milan, 'capital of the Resistance,' throughout the last months of the war. The Committee had been created in January 1944 and after the liberation of Rome and central Italy in the summer became the acknowledged leader of partisan warfare in German-occupied Italy.

On a crisp, early March morning in 1945, Major Massimo (Max William) Salvadori-Paleotti, Max Salvadori for short, had been driven into Milan by a Socialist member of the Resistance from Turin. It had been a month since the officer had parachuted into the rolling hills of the Langhe in southern Piedmont on 4 February as head of Operation Chariton.

Five men accompanied him on the mission: Captain John Keany, from County Cork, who was the second-in-command; Sergeant William (Bill) Pickering, the radio operator; Major Adrian Hope from South Africa, and his radio operator, Corporal 'Busty' Millard, both destined for a sub-mission; and finally an agent known only as Giovanni, who disappeared immediately on the landing to carry out an action with other agents of the OSS.

Bill Pickering told me that this was the third mission he had gone on with Salvadori, writing in his memoir, *The Bandits of Cisterna*: 'Soldiers cannot elect their leaders, but I could think of nobody that I would have rather followed in such a situation.' [1] The officer was six-foot tall, with brown hair, pale blue eyes, and a military moustache; he spoke perfect English with an upper class accent.

Aged 36 in March 1945, Salvadori was born in London on 16 June

1908 to noble Anglo-Italian parents, returning to Italy when just a few weeks old. In 1924, he and his philosopher father, Guglielmo, were severely beaten by Fascist thugs in Florence and the family was forced to flee to Switzerland.

Max graduated from the University of Geneva in 1929 and returned to Italy to study for his doctorate in Rome and to promote the underground *Giustizia e Libertà* movement with the codename of *Speranza* (Hope). In 1932, he was betrayed, arrested by the Fascists, and sent to prison on the island of Ponza, but thanks to the intervention of an influential British cousin was amnestied a year later.

Salvadori decided to leave the country and began what he described as his second exile, which this time would last for ten years. After farming in Kenya, he travelled widely across the Continent, including several visits to England, where in 1938 he hired a converted trawler to sail close enough to the German coast for the voice of 'Free Germany' to be heard over the radio. While the ship was in port after a few days at sea, a suspicious explosion put an untimely end to the enterprise.

Salvadori found employment in the United States as a Professor in Economics and Sociology at a New York university. Once war broke out, the British Government asked him to help organise Italian-Americans and fellow Italian exiles into an anti-fascist group and to go to Mexico to thwart Fascist sympathisers who were sending radio messages to German submarines in the Caribbean; with two other exiles he put the wireless station they were using out of action with an explosion.

On 19 January 1943, Salvadori received a telephone call from the British Consulate in Mexico City to tell him that an old application he had made to enlist in the British Army had finally been accepted and that he was to go to London as soon as possible.

Salvadori sailed from Halifax, arriving in Liverpool on 1 March.

Next day, he met Lieutenant-Colonel Cecil Roseberry, head of the Italian Section of SOE, at the War Office in London, who asked him if he would like to join Special Operations. Salvadori replied: 'Yes, on condition that I am allowed to enlist in the British Army.' He added that once in uniform he would obey orders to the best of his ability; the Colonel assured him that he could enlist at once as a private and would receive a commission after commando training.

Salvadori left England by plane for North Africa on 6 July and on the 26th he set foot on Italian soil for the first time in ten years as the 8th Army landed on Sicily. Under the alias of Max Sylvester, he became a captain in Special Force's forward detachment, codenamed Vigilant. It rescued the philosopher Benedetto Croce from Sorrento, but came to grief on the Anzio beachhead in February 1944, when Salvadori was evacuated suffering from jaundice. Once recovered, he took part in operations to insert agents into enemy territory, for which he was awarded the Military Cross.

Salvadori was promoted to major and in June was able to make a brief visit to his family home after British troops captured Fermo. On 30 October, he wrote in his diary: 'I am to act as liaison officer between 15th Army Group and the National Liberation Committee. Captain John Keany and Sergeant Pickering, a telegraphist, will accompany me. I have also asked for Giordana, whom I met here; his cooperation will be extremely valuable if I ever get to Milan.' Gian Pietro Giordana was a thirty-two-year-old journalist and Italian member of SOE.

While waiting for a suitable moment to be dropped into Piedmont, Salvadori completed his parachute training and was responsible for the first draft of what became known as the Rome Protocols. They were signed at the Grand Hotel in Rome on 7 December 1944, on behalf of the Liberation Committee by Alfredo Pizzoni, Ferruccio Parri, Giancarlo Pajetta, and Edgardo Sogno (all brought south clandestinely 'under the auspices of SOE'), and by General

Maitland Wilson for the Allies. The partisans' objectives were to obtain a degree of recognition, to ask for increased financial assistance, and to request larger supplies.

It was agreed that the Liberation Committee would act in accordance with Allied instructions and receive a monthly subsidy. It was also to nominate a military commander acceptable to the Allies. The choice had already fallen on General Raffaele Cadorna, whom the British had parachuted into the Val Cavallina in August. During the final offensive, the Committee would maintain law and order until handing over its powers to the Allied Military Government (AMG), when the partisan formations would be disbanded and their weapons surrendered.

At the end of the month, the new Italian Government of Ivanoe Bonomi also reluctantly signed up to the agreement. It delegated the Liberation Committee to represent it in the struggle in occupied Italy, and, in turn, the Committee accepted the government as the legitimate authority in the rest of the country.

The major's instructions on Operation Chariton were to coordinate the activities of the partisans with those of the Allied army; to see that supplies in sufficient quantities reached the Military Committee irrespective of political colour; to encourage the Liberation Committee to set up provincial organisations to take over the functions of public administration during an interim period; to ensure the protection of industrial plants and power stations; to prevent individuals and groups from making any agreement with the Germans; to prevent Yugoslav or French infiltration on both eastern and western fronts; and finally, to do everything possible to maintain harmony among the parties of the Liberation Committee.

Salvadori noted that the most important instruction was given orally by Special Force Commander Gerry Holdsworth: 'Do your best,' and he wrote: 'Once in enemy territory the British Liaison Officer (BLO) was on his own. Within the frame of general and vague instructions, the BLO had as guide his knowledge and appreciation of the situation and his conscience ... Politics? It was reiterated again and again that military considerations, the contribution to the Allied war effort, were the foremost concern.' Salvadori also related that apart from military activities, his job was to make suggestions, never to give orders, with the Liberation Committee acting as a sovereign body and not as a puppet.

For his stay in Milan, Salvadori relied on the young journalist, Gian Pietro Giordana. On the first day, Salvadori saw the Socialist leader, Sandro Pertini, and the Liberation Committee President, the banker Alfredo Pizzoni, newly returned from the Rome mission, who gave him the news that he had been promoted to lieutenant-colonel. Then there were meetings with the other political leaders from the five parties on the Committee: Communists, Socialists, Christian Democrats, Liberals, and Actionists.

Salvadori knew some of the men by reputation, others he had encountered before in the south. Within a few days he had also met members of the Military Committee, other partisan commanders, and members of the Liberation Committee. He recalled: 'I reckoned at the time that I met altogether about sixty people, a few only once, others several times.' He only had one meeting with Luigi Longo of the Communists, but saw General Cadorna on several occasions.

Salvadori recalled: 'I was invited to attend the meetings of the National Liberation Committee, which I did, only once, however. I did it to clarify points concerning responsibilities of the Committee during the interim period preceding the arrival of the Allied Military Government.'

The meeting, the most important one of the war, began at 8 a.m. on 25 April 1945 at the Salesiano Institute (Catholic School) in the Via Copernico in Milan. Members emerged from the rain, quickly crossed the threshold of the cloister, and entered the cold and darkened library. Priests dressed in black cassocks were watching the entrance. In his memoir, *The Labour and the Wounds*, Salvadori wrote: 'Our hearts were heavy with emotion and a burden had been lifted from our spirits. We knew that this was no ordinary day. The end was at hand; the end of the war for all men; the end of what we had been fighting against for twenty long years.' [2]

As well as giving all partisan units the order to launch the revolt against the Germans and Fascists, a decree was issued on judicial procedure under which unnamed leading Fascists would be tried, with capital punishment or life imprisonment as the sanctions.

There were ten signatures: Luigi Longo and Emilio Sereni for the Communists; Ferruccio Parri and Leo Valiani for the Actionists; Augusto De Gasperi and Achille Marazza for the Christian Democrats; Rodolfo Morandi (who replaced Alfredo Pizzoni as President on 29 March) and Sandro Pertini for the Socialists; and Giustino Arpesani and Filippo Jacini for the Liberals.

Salvadori provided valuable intelligence to base, but personal security and the lack of a radio were his immediate concerns. The risk of being caught was greatest in urban areas, so it was essential that he had a number of hideouts. Giordana, who also provided him with a bicycle, arranged for him to stay with a friend called Paolo Barioli, at 3, Via Uberto Visconti di Modrone. Unknown to all, except a member of the Liberation Committee, the Colonel also had a base in the Bruzzano district of the city, where as a fall-back he made use of the apartment of a cousin he had not seen for over 20 years called Guido Brofferio. Through Pizzoni, he was also able to use the house of an industrialist near Milan and often spent weekends there, preparing reports, eight in total, for couriers ('mainly provided by Leo Valiani') to take to Lugano.

Salvadori recalled: 'I met many people but psychologically, I was 'alone and always on the run.' Communications with the Allied Command were difficult but frequent. Still in Piedmont, Keany and Pickering had been instructed to remain in uniform and it meant restricting their movements to areas controlled by partisans. It was intended that couriers would maintain contact with them, but none sent from Milan reached their destination. There was no news until Salvadori was notified by Giordana that Captain Keany had been killed in action near Basso Monferrato on 8 March. Subsequently, a courier from Alessandria reported that Major Hope was also dead, victim of an accidental shooting on 17 April.

Salvadori was able to use four different clandestine radios to contact headquarters: one run by the OSS in Milan, another controlled by monarchist partisans east of the city, and two run by SOE missions in Liguria and Piedmont. They were all extremely cooperative and communications became easier after the dropping of other Allied missions in Lombardy. Besides providing signals and reports concerning the Liberation Committee and the partisan forces, he was asked among other things 'to check on rumours concerning the willingness of the SS commander to negotiate a German surrender in Italy, something also involving a high ranking member of the Archbishop's entourage.' This was a reference to the Secretary, Don Giuseppe Bicchierai.

Salvadori recalled: 'The end came more quickly than I expected. By March, new volunteers were flooding into the partisan formations and continual firing at night indicated that their action squads were active in the city.' On 21 April, parades, ceremonies, and speeches were held to mark the Fascist National and Labour Day, but three days later the Christian Democrat Achille Marazza and the Communist Emilio Sereni of the Liberation Committee told Salvadori about the unlikely meeting planned for the 25th between leaders of the Fascists and the Resistance.

This provided the Colonel with an ideal opportunity to capture Mussolini, as we shall see in the next chapter.

24 SOE AGENTS ~ 2

The famous meeting between Mussolini and his mortal enemies of the Italian Resistance at the Archbishop's palace in Milan on 25 April 1945 allowed leading SOE agent Max Salvadori to launch a plan to seize the dictator with inside help from moderates on the National Liberation Committee.

In an interview with journalist Silvio Bertoldi in 1962, one of its former members, Achille Marazza of the Christian Democrats, related that once the Socialist firebrand Sandro Pertini arrived at the meeting after unknowingly crossing paths with Mussolini on the steps of the Prefecture: 'He began to speak loudly, arguing that even if Mussolini had surrendered he would have to be kept for two or three days and then, instead of handing him over to the Allies, he would have had to be brought to trial.' Marazza and Riccardo Lombardi of the Action Party bitterly opposed the idea, upholding the promises made to hand over the dictator to the Allies.

Meanwhile, the Fascist ex-prefect Carlo Tiengo, who had heard everything, got up and slipped out of the room. General Renzo Montagna, former chief of the Republican Police, recalled: 'Naturally, he immediately warned him that his life was in danger, and that explains everything else.'

Writing in the Socialist newspaper, *Avanti,* on 16 April 1965, Sandro Pertini related:

It is clear that my intervention at the Cardinal's (an intervention supported only by Comrade Emilio Sereni, but very energetically) prompted Mussolini to decide against surrendering. And, above all, it is clear that if on the evening of 25 April Comrade Sereni and I had not gone to the Archbishopric, and if therefore Mussolini had surrendered to the National Liberation Committee, he would have been delivered to the British Colonel, Max Salvadori, which in fact meant handing him over to the Allies, and he would be here today at Montecitorio.

This was a reference to the palace in Rome, which is the seat of the Italian Chamber of Deputies.

In his 1962 interview, Marazza recalled what happened after the departure of Mussolini:

We waited a long time in the Archbishopric and finally telephoned the Prefecture. Prefect Bassi replied and told us that Mussolini had left. There was nothing more to wait for. Lombardi and I went out together. For my part, I took steps to warn Max Salvadori, head of the British mission, that Mussolini would no longer be surrendering to the National Liberation Committee. In fact, Salvadori had waited near the Archbishopric for the Fascist leader to surrender, to take him over, and to lead him to a place of safety. With this in mind, we had agreed that he would be accommodated at the 'Muti' barracks in Via Rovello, or, better still, in the Archbishopric itself.

In his memoir, *The Labour and the Wounds*, Salvadori related that on leaving the crucial meeting of the Liberation Committee on the morning of 25 April he went for lunch and had discussions with friends. Less than two hours later he picked up his bicycle and toured the streets to see what was going on and found a scene of great confusion, as everyone seemed to be running away. Salvadori went back to the flat at about five o'clock but did not stay there long, as he had appointments to keep:

This time I went on foot ... I reached the *prefettura*; people were rushing in and out in a great hurry. The courtyard was crowded. No one seemed to be in charge. Out of control and making a good deal of noise, in a big room on the first floor, were the last of the Fascist *gerarchi* [leaders], the last of the ministers, the last of the dictator's personal guard. Silence fell gradually as the room emptied … By nightfall only a handful of people remained in the large building.' [1]

It soon became clear that Mussolini had stormed out of the meeting and run away. Once this attempt to capture him had failed it was all over except for skirmishes next morning. Salvadori addressed the Italian nation over Milan Radio in the evening, together with the engineer Riccardo Lombardi, who was appointed the new Prefect.

On 29 April, Salvadori saw the first American patrol of two jeeps and two armoured cars roll into Piazza della Scala in the city centre. Next day, General Willis Dale Crittenberger, commander of the 4th American Army Corps, arrived and was met by United States colonel Charles Poletti, who was appointed Allied Military Governor. Lieutenant-Colonel Hedley Vincent had also arrived in the city to finalise British SOE operations.

Salvadori was made an 'Honorary Citizen' of Milan and awarded the 'Freedom of the City' in a ceremony attended by British officers and members of the Liberation Committee; Sandro Pertini made a speech. The agent would also be awarded the Distinguished Service Order (DSO) by the British, to add to his earlier Military Cross.

On 6 May, Salvadori accompanied members of the Liberation Committee to Rome. His mission was over. On leaving the army, he lectured at Smith College, Northampton, Massachusetts, becoming Professor of Modern European History. Apart from short leaves of absence in Paris to fill senior roles in UNESCO and NATO, he taught there until his retirement in 1973, writing over twenty books.

In recent years, Max Salvadori's wartime role of Liaison Officer with the Liberation Committee in Milan has come under extra scrutiny as the result of the persistent rumours of SOE involvement in the death of Mussolini, as we shall see in the next chapter.

25 SOE AGENTS ~ 3

Did an Italian partisan commander kill Mussolini on the orders of a British secret agent, who in turn executed Claretta Petacci?

In 1994 the publication of a book making these claims from major Milanese publishing house Ugo Mursia astounded all those interested in the last hours of the dictator and his lover.

The book, entitled *Quel 28 aprile, Mussolini e Claretta: la verità* (That 28 April, Mussolini and Petacci, the Truth), was written by self-confessed assassin Bruno Giovanni Lonati. He stated that he had executed Mussolini in the morning on the orders of a British secret agent known as Captain John, who had then shot Claretta Petacci because she knew too much.

Lonati said that he wrote the book in 1981, apart from a few corrections made later; until then no one ever knew about the story, even his own family. In the following year he confided in Roberto Gervaso, a writer whom he deeply respected, with the results of their conversations being incorporated without comment into that author's volume, *Claretta, La donna che morì per Mussolini* (Claretta, the Woman Who Died for Mussolini).

Lonati was born on 3 June 1921 in Legnano, a small city 20 kilometres to the north-west of Milan. He worked for the local engineering firm of Franco Tosi Meccanica before serving in the army from 1941 to 1943 and then becoming a partisan south of Varese in the Olona Valley.

After acting as Political Commissar of the 101st Garibaldi Brigade for about a year, Lonati moved to Milan in February 1945 and found lodgings near the Central Station in Via Vallazze. He adopted the role of a commercial traveller called Angelo Parini and commanded a division of three partisan brigades under the alias of Giacomo, also acting as a liaison officer on the Command of the Garibaldi Brigades Grouping of Milan and Province, which met every week.

Only identified as John, the British secret agent first appears on page 49 of the book as 'a captain in the British Army enrolled in the secret services ... under the direct command of Marshal Alexander.' Lonati added: 'He was introduced to us at a meeting of the Group Command by "Guido" [Aldo Lampredi].' The officer was tall, of slender build, with straight black hair, brown eyes, and regular features. He did not look particularly British, but often displayed their unemotional nature and calm disposition and was systematic in the way he worked.

John had been parachuted in the previous months, had meetings with some members of the Liberation Committee and had then gone to Switzerland, not having found them useful to rely on. He returned and created his own network of collaborators and informants, which branched out into almost all of Lombardy, in particular in the Varese and Como areas. 'In short, he organized the activity of a real secret service, with clear and well defined objectives.' [1]

Lonati was informed in advance of John's arrival and it was easy for him to find him a room in the guest house in Via Vallazze where he was staying, introducing him as a fellow commercial traveller. Lonati was happy to have company and their exchange of information increasingly cemented their friendship, which went far beyond that created by fighting and bearing risks together.

Lonati completed his portrait of the Briton in the remainder of the chapter. His father had emigrated to England from southern Italy early in the century, settled in London, and after becoming a simple tailor launched a men's clothing factory.

John had studied at Oxford and then followed a military career. Before the war he lived for two years in Florence and therefore spoke excellent Italian.

He participated a few times at their weekly meetings and learned of their needs, which resulted in airdrops of weapons, medicines, food, and money to partisans in the Val Sesia, Val d'Ossola, and Val

Olona. 'He listened, took note of everything, and stayed silent.'

John had fought in Normandy as a staff officer and then came to Italy. Lonati wrote:

Even if then he did not then explicitly reveal his function to me (I saw him in the uniform of captain at the beginning of May 1945), he operated within wide margins of independence and discretion. He had few direct superiors.

Once when he was away from Milan for two days, he told me that he had gone to Salò on Lake Garda and had seen Mussolini at a distance.

His commented 'A broken man, with a brutish look.' On several occasions he mentioned the probability of Mussolini finding refuge in Germany. [2]

After taking over a school in Viale Lombardia as a headquarters for his partisan division on 24 April, Lonati returned to the guesthouse and found John waiting for him:

He told me that Mussolini and all the major leaders were in Milan and added that the partisan war was now to be considered over. He also said seriously that Mussolini should be captured.

I replied: 'Someone will do it, he cannot escape.'

'We should do it,' he replied.

'As if,' I concluded.

It seemed to me that he was joking. But it was not so ... I asked him what he would do; the reply was laconic. 'Nothing for now, I'm waiting.' The next morning, we parted, after I told him where he could find me. [3]

Around four o'clock on the afternoon of 27 April, John suddenly called on Lonati at the school on Viale Lombardia. The captain was wearing a paramilitary uniform, had a large knapsack on his back, and wielded a nine calibre Beretta pistol and a Sten gun.

'You must help me, only you can do it,' he said. 'We have to pursue Mussolini and capture him.'

'Why us?'

'Because I don't see who else can do it.'

'And the others, do they know? Where does this decision come from?'

'They know nothing,' he replied, 'and I think they won't have to know anything, at least if we succeed.'

Lonati asked: 'But where is Mussolini?'

'He is in Como and intends to head towards the Valtellina with a Fascist column, but that is not certain. If we move immediately, before evening we will know where he is making for.'

'But how do you know all these things? And why are you really interested in Mussolini?'

'What's the point of winning a war if you don't capture the chief opponent?'

Lonati said: 'Mussolini will not be able to escape or to flee; with all the partisans around, I think he has already been captured.'

John replied: 'Stop talking and follow me. What are you doing among these people?'

Lonati was caught off guard and wanted to think about it, but was eventually persuaded to go. He asked 'Who are we taking with us?'

'At least two or three of your most trusted men.' And after a pause: 'Have you got a car?'

'Yes, it's down in the street.' It was a Fiat 1100 in good condition that they had requisitioned from a doctor some days earlier.

'Let's go then.'

John, Lonati and three other partisans - only identified as Bruno, Gino, and Lino - drove to a rendezvous with an agent who revealed where Mussolini and Petacci were being held. He directed them to a villa at Brunate, above Como, where they spent the night, and in the morning told them the way to the house at Bonzanigo.

Lino was killed when their car ran through a partisan roadblock on the outskirts of Argegno, but at about 10.30 on the morning of the 28th rest of the party arrived at the De Maria house. The guards were disarmed and Lonati led the way up the stairs.

Mussolini was standing and Petacci was sitting on the edge of the bed.

John brusquely asked the dictator 'Where are the papers?'

'What papers?'

'Your papers, don't act the fool.'

'But I only have this this briefcase,' he said, indicating a large one lying on the floor that was torn and made of brown leather.

John threw it onto the bed and began to check the contents. Mussolini said: 'But these are only my writings, there's nothing important, nothing that could interest you.'

'We'll see. We'll see,' John replied. But eventually finding that they were only a collection of Mussolini's notes and articles, he asked: 'But didn't you have other papers?'

'Yes,' replied Mussolini, 'and very important ones too, but they were taken by the others last night.'

'Who were they?'

'I don't remember the names, I've heard so many names, Pedro, Pietro, and others as well, and then there was a woman too. I told them that they were historic documents, which would have explained many things to the world and which I wanted to hand to the Allies, but they snatched the bag from my hand and told me it would be safer in their hands. They also told me I would get it back.'

Lonati went out onto the landing with John and asked: 'What must we do?'

'We have to shoot them.'

'Petacci as well?'

'Yes, Petacci as well.'

'Why, what does she have to do with it?'

'I think that we have to do it because she knows many of Mussolini's secrets, because perhaps she knows the content of the papers, and because no one knows where they are. And then if we don't do it, the others will.'

Lonati said that he could not shoot Petacci, but John said that he would take care of her, adding that Mussolini would have to be shot by an Italian.

The couple were marched for about two hundred metres, pushed down a side track, and machine gunned to death while they were leaning against a wire fence.

They partially covered the bodies in Mussolini's overcoat.

Lonati said: 'Let's go.'

It was a little after eleven on 28 April.

In the following days, Lonati and his men only saw John on a couple of occasions. On 2 May, the day the war in Italy officially ended, Lonati returned from a visit to his home in Legnano and learned that the British authorities were looking for him in connection with the disappearance of a leading Fascist prisoner snatched from his men's custody by another partisan group.

Lonati went to Via Moscova, where the British had established their headquarters. He was interrogated by the commander, who kept on repeating 'I want to know where that man is,' while he kept answering: 'I don't know.'

Suddenly, there was a knock at the door and John appeared.

At first Lonati did not recognise him. He was wearing an impeccable uniform and quickly shook his hand and embraced him, much to the amazement of the commander. Lonati explained his reason for being there and John was successful in making his superior understand his friend's good faith and truthfulness. As the

Briton accompanied Lonati to the entrance he again recommended him to keep their mission secret.

Lonati recalled: 'I asked him about the papers and documents, which had tormented him so much: he was very vague, as if the matter did not greatly interest him. He had high hopes, but did not add anything more.'

John also told him that his mission in Italy was coming to an end and that in four weeks he would be returning to Britain. He wanted to see them before leaving and gave Lonati his telephone number, asking him to call before 20 May.

Lonati recalled that they arranged a farewell dinner, which was also attended by Gino and Bruno. There he was given a flat, metal box containing a document that stated that he had rendered notable services to the United Kingdom. If ever he found himself in difficulty he could show it to the British authorities to summon aid, but only in case of emergency. He wrote: 'This document was only issued to me. Naturally, I have never used it; I don't think I ever will.'

Lonati asked John about Mussolini's famous missing papers. He replied: 'Better not to talk about them.' Lonati recalled: 'I didn't insist any more. I am curious, but have always remembered the old Milanese maxim: 'The less you know the better off you are.'

John said that for military and ethical reasons whatever had happened had to stay a secret, no matter what others said. Lonati recalled him emphasising: 'According to a British code of honour we had to keep quiet for at least 35 years, after which we would be free to say what really happened. He also said that only after 50 years could we have irrefutable proofs by consulting the British Archives, as everything had been written and documented.'

Two years after the publication of his book, Lonati decided to add some details to his account in a 24-page document entitled 'An Unfinished Story,' which was handed to the editor of Italian magazine *Storia Illustrata* (History Illustrated) and then passed to author Luciano Garibaldi.

It stated that 15 years earlier, in July 1981, Lonati had spoken on the telephone to John's brother, 'Mr X,' who was manager of a large London retail store. He said that John was in Canada. Lonati left his telephone number and a few days later was surprised to receive a call from his wartime companion.

He told him that he was still connected to the services and had even become one of the heads. He added that the documents that concerned Lonati were in good hands and confirmed that once the 50-year limit had passed, his country's authorities would release them to him. The Italian replied that once 35 years had gone by he intended to go public by telling the story to a reputable scholar. John said he had no problem with that and that he could do as he wished.

They arranged a meeting at the Royal Lancaster Hotel in London for the first week of August and Lonati duly arrived there with his wife, but there was no sign of John. A Coventry telephone number he had given them also proved to be false. However, when they returned to the hotel on the 12th they found a message from him, saying that he had been unable to come to the capital, but would be in Italy at the end of the month. Lonati wrote ruefully: 'From then on I never again had any contact with or news from him.'

In a final attempt to contact the British before handing over his notes to author Roberto Gervaso, Lonati said that he paid a visit to the Consul in Milan, Mr P. H. P. Thompson, on 2 February 1982, and showed him his text. Lonati recounted: 'The Consul authorised me to give the notes to Gervaso for publication in his book and together we wrote the draft of a letter saying that at the fifty-year limit the British authorities would release the documents to me.' Lonati also said that he wrote to the British Ambassador to Italy, Sir Patrick Fairweather, on 8 June 1995, again asking for the documents. No answer was received.

Ten years after Lonati's book was published, the author and former OSS agent Peter Tompkins, who between 1942 and 1945 served in Algeria, Naples, Rome, and Berlin (but never in northern Italy), produced two television documentaries in support of the ex-partisan's claims with his wife Maria Luisa Forenza. Entitled 'Mussolini, the Final Truth,' and 'The Churchill-Mussolini Correspondence: the Final Truth,' the programmes were aired on the Italian channel RAI 3 on two evenings in August and September 2004. Lonati was the main witness. Tompkins described John as 'A British officer of SOE sent by Marshal Alexander.'

The documentaries claimed that the post-war painting trips to the Italian lakes by Winston Churchill were cover for attempts to retrieve his correspondence with Mussolini. The programmes also stated that the real name of the famous 'Captain John' was Robert Maccarrone (or Maccaroni), which he was said to have later changed to Mcroney.

In light of the television accounts, the British newspapers *The Times* and *The Independent* followed the lead of mainstream Italian titles in featuring Lonati's story, while both maintaining a sceptical tone. [4] The truthfulness of Lonati's narrative rests on him actually being 'a witness and protagonist of the event,' as described on the cover of his book, but it lacks supporting evidence.

There is a complete lack of witnesses. He was never able to track down the famous 'Captain John,' despite saying (in his 1996 document, but not in his 1994 book) that he went to London and arranged an appointment with him, which, however, was never kept. Lonati said in the document that he also went in search of his two surviving partisans, known only as Bruno and Gino, for confirmation of his journey, but again without result.

In his book, Lonati wrote that in 1981 he visited Lia De Maria at Bonzanigo, but that, 'She was forced to keep silent or, with the typical cunning of peasants and mountain people, she preferred to keep silent to have a quiet life, also considering that in the weeks and months following the events many people disappeared.' [5] Finally, he said that the other inhabitants of the hamlet had accepted the official story in a 'fatal slumber of collective intelligence and consciousness.' [6]

There are several other doubtful claims and useful coincidences in Lonati's story, including the fact of being bound by a British code of honour that obliged him to keep silent for 35 years, and then having to wait for another 15 years before looking for proofs in the United Kingdom National Archives.

What is most dubious is the claim that a British secret agent, 'Captain John,' would be introduced at a weekly meeting of the provincial command of the Garibaldi Brigades by Aldo Lampredi, right-hand man of the Communist leader, Luigi Longo. Just as unbelievable is the idea of John attaching himself to an unknown twenty-three-year old partisan officer, giving him all the details of his military background, and involving him in a top secret operation.

As described by Lonati, the Briton was also a very busy man, not only arranging the mission, but creating his own network of collaborators and informants across 'almost all of Lombardy,' as well as arranging supply airdrops to meet the vast needs of partisans in three strategic areas for the imminent rising.

Lonati was undoubtedly a fine partisan officer, but did he kill Mussolini on the orders of a British secret agent, who in turn executed Claretta Petacci?

In one word, no.

26 ALLIED ORDERS

Allied policy on the fate of Mussolini and his leading followers was precise and long-standing. It was set out in Article 29 of the Long Armistice of 29 September 1943. The document was signed on the British battleship HMS *Nelson* in Grand Harbour, Malta, by General Dwight D. Eisenhower for the Allies and by Marshal Pietro Badoglio for the Royalist Italian Government. The article read:

Benito Mussolini, his Chief Fascist associates and all persons suspected of having committed war crimes or analogous offences whose names appear on lists to be communicated by the United Nations will forthwith be apprehended and surrendered into the hands of the United Nations. Any instructions given by the United Nations for this purpose will be complied with. [1]

On the day of Mussolini's execution, 28 April 1945, the Allies had bombarded the National Liberation Committee in Milan with a series of increasingly desperate secret cablegrams.

The Committee was based in the former headquarters of the Army Corps in Via Brera. Its radio service was run by Giuseppe Cirillo (Ettore), with the assistance of Agostino Cesareo (Aurelio). Both were former merchant navy operators and employees of Marconi until volunteering for the 'Otto' Resistance network based in Genoa, which was run by SOE.

Arrested when the cell was destroyed at the end of March 1944 by the German security service, the *Sicherheitsdienst (SD),* they eventually escaped from prison and resumed their clandestine activities in the new setting of Milan.

On 28 April, the operators received three urgent messages from the OSS Secret Intelligence base located in the Villa Strozzi in Florence. The first, numbered 74, was signed by Max Corvo. It read:

The 15th Army Group wishes to have Mussolini and Graziani brought to its Headquarters. If you are willing to release them, it will be possible to send an aircraft. Please let us know where it is possible to land a four-engine plane to pick them up.

The landing ground would probably have been the military airport of Bresso, only eight kilometres to the north of Milan city centre, as the Headquarters in Siena had proposed it as a location on the previous evening. Corvo's message to the Resistance leaders went unanswered, so a more detailed one, numbered 75, was sent from Florence, this time signed by both Captain Arthur Latina and agent 'Smith':

The Allied Command desires to receive immediate information on the location of Mussolini and orders that he be held for immediate transport to the Allied Command. You have to ascertain where he is to be found and to notify the above-mentioned order to partisans who could have him in their hands. This order has to be given the utmost priority.

Cirillo recalled that he passed the message on to Major Mario Argenton, one of two adjutants on the Military Committee. Also present was its commander, General Raffaele Cadorna, and Sandro Pertini, Socialist member of the Liberation Committee. Once again there was no reply and Latina and 'Smith' were forced to follow up their message with a longer one. Cablegram number 86 read:

The Allied Command issues the following orders: 1. Send immediate information concerning the location in which Mussolini is now to be found. 2. Hold him for transfer to the Allied Command. 3. Inform the partisan unit holding him of this. 4. Provide immediate information on an airport able to allow the landing of a two-engine and a four-engine plane. Provide information on the landing field and assurances on the possible presence of mines.

This message from the Allies finally brought a prompt reply from the partisans at the headquarters, which was a pack of lies:

The Military Committee for Allied Force Headquarters: Unfortunately, not able to hand over Mussolini; tried by the People's Court, he has been shot at the same place as fifteen patriots were shot earlier by the Nazi-Fascists. Stop.

The reference was to the Piazzale Loreto, where on 10 August 1944 fifteen partisan hostages taken from the San Vittore prison were shot by Fascist militia on the orders of the Germans.

As Leo Valiani of the Liberation Committee would admit later, at the last minute it was absolutely necessary 'to avoid the intrusion of the Allies.' The blatant falsehood they used to bring this about succeeding in opening the way for the plan of the Insurrectional Committee to pick up Mussolini and to kill him to be put into effect.

On the penultimate day of the war in Italy, 1 May 1945, radio operator Giuseppe Cirillo sent his last message to Allied Force Headquarters. Numbered 652, it read:

From the head of the Milan radio service to the head of radio service at base: As the liberation of northern Italy has taken place, this radio service, which has always worked in difficult conditions, is closing; we wish to remember the fallen operatives and thank you and all your operators for your constant support and assistance in all our difficulties. Hurrah.

The sun was about to shine on a peaceful land.

27 GENERAL CADORNA'S ORDERS

The weight of Allied orders concerning the fate of Mussolini fell most heavily on the shoulders of General Raffaele Cadorna, who had been parachuted into northern Italy in August 1944 by the British as 'a safe pair of hands' to spearhead the partisan war as leader of the military committee.

Once the partisan mission to capture and execute Mussolini and his leading followers was being planned, the General launched one of his own in line with Allied policy to save him. Its success would have completely frustrated the aims of his more radical comrades.

After hearing from the Allies in Siena that a plane could be available at the military airport of Bresso to take delivery of Mussolini, Cadorna telephoned his aide-de-camp, Lieutenant-Colonel Baron Giovanni Sardagna of Hohenstein, newly appointed military leader of the Resistance in the Como area and formerly his companion in the defence of Rome in 1943.

The Baron was told to find a refuge in which to hold Mussolini safely for a few hours until he could be taken into custody by the Allied troops arriving from the south and eventually put before a regular tribunal.

As part of this plan, a senior agent of the United States Counter-Intelligence Corps (CIC), John McDonough, attached to the advancing 1st Armored Division, sent Sardagna an urgent telegram once he arrived in Como: 'Mussolini and Graziani are to be brought to Blevio for the disposition of the American police.' The village is a few kilometres from Como on the eastern shore of the lake.

Sardagna noted in his diary that General Cadorna sent him a series of urgent messages on 27 April requesting that he save Mussolini and hand him over to the Counter-Intelligence Corps. By late evening, the Baron had put a plan into action, though personally he thought that it had little chance of success.

He wrote: 'I have to involve friends and trusted people, but equally I have great difficulty in explaining myself to Pedro [Count Pier Luigi Bellini delle Stelle], not because he does not understand the situation, but because he is held back by some of his own men.'

Sardagna telephoned his friend Remo Cademartori, a cheese industry magnate and owner of a villa in Blevio, which was hidden in tree-lined grounds and equipped with its own landing stage. Cademartori agreed to send a boat across the lake to Moltrasio to collect Mussolini under cover of darkness and to bring him to the villa.

To complete the plan, Sardagna telephoned the Count and gave him the order to drive Mussolini back south to Moltrasio after completely bandaging his head in such a way as to ensure that no one would recognise him on the journey.

However, at one in the morning on the 28th, Cadorna telephoned the Baron to inform him that the operation was being suspended and to beg him to find a temporary refuge for the dictator in the vicinity of Como. Sardagna noted in his diary that the scheme had failed miserably because no one had shown up in Moltrasio.

He wrote: 'I do not know what could have happened; indeed, I have thousands of doubts and fears. As for the rest, a great confusion has reigned here since yesterday; Cadorna is often contradictory and while some would be favourable to the handing over of Mussolini to McDonough as promised, others are totally opposed.'

As we have seen, the real reason for the failure of the plan was that the two cars carrying Mussolini and Petacci on the night of 27-28 April were forced to turn back after the partisans thought they heard gunfire when they reached Moltrasio. They had then driven back north along the Via Regina as far as the De Maria house in Bonzanigo, where the couple spent their last night.

Later on the 28th, the Baron wrote in his diary: 'This morning they sent us a certain "Valerio," who has an impressive pass and the tasks of reaching Mussolini and bringing him back. I have ensured that he is accompanied by two of our own men [Cosimo Maria De Angelis and Oscar Sforni] and hopefully this is the right move.'

However, in concluding his account, Sardagna wrote on 29 April: 'Mussolini was executed together with the captured leaders. It seems that "Valerio" was tasked with the execution; our own men could not prevent it, as they were locked up until late evening.'

In a twist in the tale, General Cadorna revealed in his memoir, *La Riscossa* (The Rising), first published in 1948, that he had opposed the idea of a trial for Mussolini all along:

Faced with the necessity of acting immediately and with the impossibility of making direct contact with the National Liberation Committee, which did not sit permanently, I acted as I always did during my life as a soldier, only asking myself what would be best for Italy regardless of my own personal concerns. Would the capture of Mussolini by the Allies and the consequent spectacular trial, which would inevitably become the examination of Italian politics over more than 20 years, have helped? At the time it was necessary to remain silent on facts and circumstances in which it would be extremely difficult to separate the responsibilities of a people from those of a leader. Who could presume that after so much discredit, Mussolini's survival could still be useful to the country?

In no circumstances then would I have voluntarily proceeded to carry out the delivery of Mussolini into the hands of the Allies so that he could be judged and executed by the foreigner. [1]

In the next chapter, we shall see that his attitude was also widely shared by many other leading members of the Resistance.

28 PARTISAN ORDERS

On 10 April 1945, the Italian Communist Party issued Directive Number 16 ahead of the final conflict.
The text read:

1. Procedure: Partisan formations will attack and eliminate Nazi-Fascist headquarters and carry out the liberation of cities, towns, and villages. Action squads will break up road blocks and wipe out Nazi-Fascist command posts. The appropriate organisations will proclaim a general strike whose character must be clearly and unmistakably defined: It must be made plain from the start that this strike is not a mere popular demonstration of anger, but the culmination of the people's long campaign for freedom and the expression of their unshakable determination.
2. Disintegration of the Enemy: The enemy will be faced with the following alternatives: 'Surrender or Die.'
3. The Struggle against a Wait-and-See Attitude: On no account whatsoever must our comrades in military or civil organisations accept any proposal or advice or consider any plan designed to limit, prevent, or obstruct the national uprising. A combination of firmness, tact, and skill must be employed in all discussions with Allied Military Missions which have elected to be the mouthpiece of those with a wait-and-see attitude, and are therefore inclined to attach too little importance to our urgent requests for the arms and ammunition needed to ensure the success of the insurrection. In the circumstances, we must be prepared to face the fact that the Allies may decide for one reason or another to withhold their support, instead of making the contribution for which we have asked.

The aims set out in the document were fully supported by the National Liberation Committee, which immediately issued its own manifestos along similar lines, one on the 19th being entitled 'Surrender or Die.' This rigid attitude was carried forward to the decisions taken by the Committee at its most important secret meeting of the war at the Salesian Institute in Milan on the morning of 25 April 1945.

After announcing the start of the rising under their leadership, the members of the Committee set out rules on the administration of justice. Article Five read:

The members of the Fascist Government and Fascist leaders guilty of having suppressed constitutional guarantees, destroyed the people's freedoms, created the Fascist regime, compromised and betrayed the fate of the country, bringing it to the present catastrophe, are to be punished with the death penalty and in lesser cases with life imprisonment.

The objects of the decree were unnamed - no doubt reflecting the fact that the members of the Committee had differing views on the matter - but it was obvious that the first target would be Mussolini and his leading supporters.

Article Fifteen required the creation of special entities to judge the accused, including War Tribunals, which were to be set up in every province, consisting of a magistrate, a war commissar, and two ordinary partisans.

None of these bodies were mentioned in the Constitution of the Kingdom of Italy or in the laws issued by the Rome Government. In addition, as we have seen, the measures conflicted with Article 29 of the Long Armistice of 29 September 1943 between the Italian Government and the Allies, as well as with the military and political agreements contained in the Rome Protocols of December 1944, which acknowledged the subordination of the Liberation Committee to Allied Force Headquarters and the Italian Government.

Walter Audisio claimed to have acted in the exercise of full powers given to him by the General Command; to have simply followed the orders of his superior, Luigi Longo; and to have done nothing more than apply Article Five of the decree of the Liberation Committee, which set capital punishment or life imprisonment as the penalties for Fascist crimes.

In his memoir, Audisio also argued that his meeting with the leaders of the 52nd partisan brigade at Dongo on 28 April was equivalent to the provisions of Article Fifteen of the Liberation Committee's document on the formation of provincial tribunals of war. He stated that 'the words spoken were few, every decision was approved, and we only had to put them into effect.'

At a hearing on 22 May 1957 of the Padua trial on the 'Gold of Dongo,' the President asked General Cadorna, who was appearing as a witness, if the military committee had given Audisio the order to eliminate Mussolini.

The General replied:

Valerio and Guido showed up on the afternoon of 27 April saying that they had been told of the capture of Mussolini and that they had been commissioned to execute him on the basis of the order already issued by the National Liberation Committee, which involved the capture and immediate shooting of all the leaders. So the sentence had existed for some time; afterwards, with a communiqué, the National Liberation Committee appropriated to itself the immediate application of the sentence of death, which had been given by an Insurrectional Committee established within the body. [1]

Luigi Longo, also heard as a witness at the hearing, confirmed that the shooting of Mussolini and the other leaders took place following a sentence of death issued by the Liberation Committee after the insurrection of 25 April. He added that the Committee had also received the proxy of the Government of Rome to conduct the partisan war without any other directives and to act on its own initiative.

The Communist (or 'the official') version of the dynamics leading to the executions was also set out in a compelling account by one of the leading participants in the partisan rising in Milan, Giovanni Pesce, in his memoir, *Quando cessarono gli spari* (When the Shooting Stopped), with a foreword by Luigi Longo, published in 1977.

Pesce was born at Visone d'Acqui in Piedmont on 22 February 1918 and migrated with his family to France, where he spent his childhood and adolescence. In 1936 he volunteered to join the International Brigades in Spain and fought in all the great battles of the Civil War, being wounded three times.

Returning to Italy in 1940, Pesce was arrested and imprisoned in Turin and later on the island of Ventotene. Liberated in August 1943 after the overthrow of Mussolini, he joined the partisan movement and as a result of his leadership in Turin and Milan was awarded the Italian Gold Medal for Military Valour.

Writing on the last hours of Mussolini in Chapter Four of his book, Pesce stated that, in contrast to the many speculative accounts, he was sticking to the facts, based on the testimonies of the participants in the mission. Beginning with the events of 27 April, his account read:

The message arrived at the General Command of the Military Committee (the CVL) in Milan from Lieutenant-Colonel Luigi Villani announcing: 'Mussolini, Pavolini, and other leaders have been arrested.' More news followed, then silence for two hours. Finally, the names of the other leaders arrested by partisans of the 52nd Garibaldi Brigade Luigi Clerici arrived.

The General Command of the CVL decided on a line to take immediately after the first message. It was General Cadorna himself who sustained the necessity of Mussolini and his leading supporters (who had not surrendered to the insurgent forces even when the negotiations instigated by Cardinal Schuster were taking place) being executed as war criminals.

It must be taken into account that the prevailing sentiment at this time was 'Surrender or Die.' All the enemies, all those responsible for the Italian catastrophe and the war that convulsed Europe and the whole world would have to pay for their sins. The leaders of the criminal Nazi-Fascists would therefore either have to surrender and submit themselves to the judgement of the Allied military forces or be executed on the spot.

The decision of the General Command of the CVL responded to a harsh reality of war.

At a meeting of the CVL in Cadorna's office at 3 p.m. on 27 April, Longo had already said: 'If Mussolini is captured by the partisans he must be dealt with immediately, in a brutal way, without trial, without theatrically, and without historic phrases.'

The Italian people had pronounced the sentence some time previously; it was only a question of carrying it out. Everyone was in agreement. Naturally, the execution of the condemned man could not be left to a peripheral command. To avoid any future doubt, it was necessary that a direct emissary of the General Command should carry it out. A commandant was chosen on whose capacity no one had any doubts: Colonel Valerio. The men to bring the operation to fruition with him would have to be equally trustworthy; and so the name of Guido (Aldo Lampredi) emerged. Naturally, an escort of trustworthy men was also needed. [2]

Proceeding to the meeting between Walter Audisio and Count Pier Luigi Bellini delle Stelle on the afternoon of 28 April in the town hall in Dongo, Pesce wrote:

After a discussion that became heated, Valerio reported that he had been ordered by the Military Committee to execute the Fascist leaders on the basis of Article Five of the National Liberation Committee's decree...

Pedro provided Valerio with the list of the captives and in agreement they compiled a list of seventeen leaders. The command was convened to act as a War Tribunal under the presidency of Colonel Valerio (Walter Audisio) and composed as follows: Guido (Aldo Lampredi); Pedro (Pier Luigi Bellini delle Stelle); Pietro Gatti (Michele Moretti), Commissar of the 52nd brigade; Bill (Urbano Lazzaro), Vice-Political Commissar. So, at 3.45 p.m., Mussolini and Petacci left their last dwelling and were taken by car to the hamlet of Mezzegra. At 4.10 p.m., justice was done. [3]

Of course, the meeting lacked a magistrate or a commissar of war, as required by the article, there was no agreed outcome - the local partisans opposed the mission - and the hasty killing at Mezzegra lacked the character of a punishment of someone found guilty by a regular tribunal.

However, whatever the merits of all of these arguments, in several court cases after the war the Italian magistrates always declared that the killing of Mussolini by the partisans had taken place during the period of enemy occupation and so was not an arbitrary execution but 'an act of war.'

29 WHO ORDERED THE KILLINGS?

Four individuals ordered the immediate execution of Mussolini and his leading supporters. This was against the wishes of many of their comrades, who believed that Walter Audisio (Colonel Valerio) was simply bringing the dictator back alive to hand over to the Allies in Milan.

On 30 March 1945, an Insurrectional Committee had been formed within the executive body of the Resistance, the National Liberation Committee, 'to overcome the indecision of those who did not have faith in the popular rising.' The new committee was only composed of members from the left-wing parties: two Communists, a Socialist, and an Actionist.

Its make-up reflected the superiority of these parties in the armed resistance. As Leo Valiani noted in his memoir, *Tutte le strade conducono a Roma* (All Roads Lead to Rome), the Communist and the Justice and Liberty formations allied to the Action Party alone represented more than 70 per cent of the total. The leftists were even stronger in the cities and from 24 April the workers in large and small industries in Milan became the driving force of the rising.

The first member of the Insurrectional Committee, Luigi Longo, was born at Fubine Monferrato in Piedmont on 15 March 1900 to a family of small landowners who moved to Turin to open a wine shop. He was called up for military service when in his first year as a student at the local polytechnic. After already making a reputation for himself as a young Socialist, Longo joined the Communist Party in 1921. He was arrested twice and fled to Paris in 1926 following the introduction of Fascist Special Laws.

Longo was given responsibility for liaison with fellow Communists among the Italian exiles and spent several months in Moscow, where he met Stalin and the other Kremlin leaders. In 1933 he became a political member of the Communist International, known as *Comintern,* and left France three years later to fight in the International Brigades during the Spanish Civil War. Longo was given important military and political roles and was wounded in the Battle of Alarcón. Under the pseudonym of Gallo he was finally appointed Inspector-General of the brigades by the Spanish Government, but left the country with the remaining volunteers in early 1939 following the defeat of the Republican cause. He was interned at Vernet by the French Government and in 1941 was handed over to the Italian police and detained on the island of Ventotene 'for Communist activity in Italy and abroad.'

Longo was freed following the overthrow of the Fascist regime in the summer of 1943 and moved to Rome. After the public announcement of the Armistice on 8 September, he became a member of the command of the Garibaldi Brigades, the partisan formations belonging to the Communist Party, and remained closely allied to its Secretary, Palmiro Togliatti, and to the Soviet Union of Stalin. In the spring of 1944, under the alias of Italo, Longo joined the military and liberation committees in the north as the area's Communist leader and commander of the Garibaldi brigades.

In August, General Raffaele Cadorna was parachuted from the south to become commandant of the military committee. At the end of the year, the Communist Longo and the Actionist Ferruccio Parri were confirmed as its Vice-Commandants, the Socialist Giovanni Battista Stucchi as Chief of Staff, and the Liberal Mario Argenton and the Christian Democrat Enrico Mattei as adjutants.

However, Parri was arrested by the German secret police in January 1945 after returning from the mission to meet the Allies in the south. In addition, General Cadorna handed in his resignation to the Liberation Committee in February following a disagreement with Parri's temporary replacement, Fermo Solari (who himself was wounded and captured by the Fascists in March).

Parri was released from jail in Verona after two months

imprisonment as a result of the secret peace negotiations in Switzerland between representatives of the Allies and the Germans in Italy. Cadorna returned to duty on the insistence of the Allies and the Rome Government, but only resumed command in Milan during the final days of the insurrection.

During all these crises, Longo remained at the helm as the most powerful military leader of the Resistance. At the end of the war, he was decorated with the American Bronze Star and went on to became a Parliamentary Deputy and, in turn, Vice-Secretary, Secretary, and finally President of the Communist Party.

Fellow party member of the Insurrectional Committee, Emilio Sereni, was born in Rome to an intellectual Jewish family on 13 August 1907. As a high school student he studied Marxism and in 1926 joined the Communist Party. A year later, Sereni graduated in agronomy at Portici, near Naples, and in 1930 went to Paris, where he met Palmiro Togliatti and other Communist leaders. He returned to Italy but was arrested by the Fascists in September and condemned to 15 years imprisonment by a Special Tribunal, where he was described as 'inflexible and a lost cause.'

Amnestied in 1935, Sereni returned to Paris clandestinely and became editor of two expatriate publications. However, owing to his position as an intellectual and a critic, he came under suspicion from other party members in 1937 during the Stalinist terror in Russia.

Sereni was condemned to death, but pardoned after writing a letter of self-criticism to the Russian leader, though he was then expelled from the party hierarchy; he moved to Toulouse and in 1941 was part of a commission to unify the activities of the Communist, Socialist, and Action parties, a precursor of the national liberation committees.

Sereni made contact with the anti-Fascist movement and created the newspaper *La parola del soldato* (The Voice of the Soldier), aimed at troops of the Italian army in the occupied zone of France.

Arrested in 1943, he was imprisoned in Antibes and tortured.

Sereni appeared before a military tribunal and was condemned to 18 years imprisonment on charges of 'the direction of civil war and incitement to desertion.' Held at Fossano in the province of Cuneo, he then fell into the hands of the SS, but survived seven months on death row in Turin by concealing his true identity. In August 1944, Sereni managed to escape to Milan. He joined Longo as the Communist representative on the Liberation Committee and was also responsible for the party's press and propaganda activities.

The Socialist member of the Insurrectional Committee was Alessandro (popularly known as Sandro) Pertini, who was born in the small mountain commune of Stella, Savona, on 25 September 1896. After serving as an officer with a machine gun unit during the First World War he embarked on a legal career, but in 1925 was arrested and sentenced to eight months imprisonment for writing a Socialist publication, which was followed by a further term of five years in 1926.

Pertini escaped and took refuge in Milan, and then in France, where he was given political asylum and worked in various labouring jobs. Returning to Italy in 1929, he was rearrested and sentenced to ten years and nine months in prison by the Special Court for the Defence of the State. He served seven years and was then sentenced to another term of eight years, but refused to ask for a pardon, even when the request was signed by his mother.

Once free again in August 1943 following the overthrow of Mussolini, Pertini joined the executive of the Socialist Party and the Liberation Committee in Rome, but was soon recaptured by the Fascists, transferred to the SS section of the Regina Coeli prison, sentenced to death, and held awaiting execution. However, he escaped in January 1944, together with another Socialist leader, Giuseppe Saragat, and became a party representative on the Liberation Committee in Milan.

Following the Liberation, Sandro Pertini received the Italian Gold Medal for Military Valour (the highest award) and became a successful journalist and politician, culminating in his role as President of the Italian Republic from 1978 to 1985, following which he was made a 'Senator for Life.'

The fourth and final member of the Insurrectional Committee was representative of the Action Party, Leo Valiani, who was born Leo Weiczen on 9 February 1909 to a Hungarian Jewish family in Fiume, an Adriatic city then part of the Austro-Hungarian Empire, which was annexed by Italy in 1924 and is now known as Rijeka in Croatia. He moved to Milan and changed his surname to Valiani. Arrested in 1928, he was sentenced to eight months imprisonment and a year's exile to the island of Ponza for 'the 'possession of anti-fascist newspapers, the instigation of civil war, and subversive propaganda.'

While in prison, Valiani joined the Communist Party after coming under the influence of its members among fellow captives. On his release he continued his clandestine activities and was soon re-arrested. On 23 June 1931, Valiani was sentenced to 12 years and 7 months imprisonment, which he served in four different prisons until amnestied in 1936. He moved to Paris and was appointed editor of the party's weekly, *Il grido del popolo* (The Cry of the People). In September, Valiani went to Spain to help Luigi Longo organise the first Italian contingent of the International Brigades. When he returned to France in the summer of 1937, he became editor of *La voce degli italiani* (The Voice of the Italians), which supported the politics of the Popular Front.

However, after the signing of the Molotov-Ribbentrop non-aggression pact between Germany and the Union of Soviet Socialist Republics (USSR) on 23 August 1939, the French Government of Daladier took action against the Italian Communist exiles. Valiani was interned in the camp at Vernet, where his critical comments to fellow prisoners led to his expulsion from the party in 1940. Fortunately, he was able to leave the camp in October with the help of some leaders of the Justice and Liberty organisation among the captives.

Valiani embarked for French Morocco with fellow exiles and from there reached Mexico. Max Salvadori, who was also in the country, recalled that after his old application to join the British Army had been accepted in early 1943, Valiani and other friends approached him with a request:

They want me to help them to get back to Europe to carry on the work interrupted by the German invasion. They are tired of the increasing quarrels and arguments among the small group of Italian anti-fascist exiles here. I have done what was possible, but without much success; only four or five of them will be helped to reach England, from where they will make their way to occupied Europe. [1]

Valiani was infiltrated behind the lines and arrived in Rome from southern Italy on 9 September as the Germans occupied the city. He joined the Action Party and was sent to Milan as their Secretary for Upper Italy. On 3 November he accompanied his party colleague Ferruccio Parri in a meeting with John McCaffery of SOE and Allen Dulles of OSS at a villa near Lugano in Switzerland. This marked the beginning of their alliance, but, as Valiani noted: 'The Allies expected only actions of sabotage and military intelligence from us … On the other hand, they were perplexed in the face of the plan for true and proper partisan warfare.'

Valiani replaced Ferruccio Parri as the party's representative on the Liberation Committee in June 1944. At the end of October, together with Alfredo Pizzoni, 'banker of the Resistance,' he took part in a meeting with Colonel Cecil Roseberry and John McCaffery of SOE in Switzerland. It was agreed that the Italians would send the delegation south to formalise military operations with the Allies and political links with the Rome Government. The agreements known as 'Rome Protocols' were the result.

In a 'Report on the Liberation Committee,' dated 31 October 1944, Roseberry wrote: 'The Allies should support the CLNAI whilst maintaining close liaison to ensure operational control.'

In the spring of 1945, Valiani accompanied General Cadorna and Ferruccio Parri to represent the Liberation Committee in meetings with senior officers from Allied Force Headquarters in Switzerland, and then in Lyons, to examine the imminent offensive on the Gothic Line and the plan for the national rising.

After the war, Valiani was a member of the Consultative Assembly, but retired from active politics with the dissolution of the Action Party in 1947. He became a prolific writer and columnist and on 1 December 1980 his wartime colleague, Sandro Pertini, by now Italian President, conferred on him the honour 'Senator for Life' of the Italian Republic.

It is clear that all four members of the Insurrectional Committee shared backgrounds that led them to develop a deep hatred of Fascists and Fascism. They were finally able to channel this feeling into ordering Mussolini's immediate execution.

30 THE ITALIAN SOLUTION

Transfers of power in dictatorships are seldom peaceful and in April 1945 Mussolini faced both advancing Allied armies and an internal partisan rising. After the failure of the attempt to negotiate an 'honourable surrender' with the Resistance at the Archbishop's palace in Milan on the 25th he decided to cut and run.

Both the British and American military authorities knew of Mussolini's movements and deployed a large number of secret agents to hunt him down and to capture him. This was in line with Allied orders and precise instructions to their men.

However, there is no evidence that an Italian partisan commander killed Mussolini on the orders of a British agent, who in turn executed Claretta Petacci, as claimed by Bruno Giovanni Lonati.

His story is typical of the many alternative theories that have emerged over the years to challenge the historical version of the death of Mussolini and Petacci. These accounts all tend to suggest that the couple were killed by a parallel mission in or near the De Maria house between dawn and midday on 28 April, often with the stated motivation to recover the fabled 'Churchill-Mussolini correspondence.'

However, faced with the reality of Walter Audisio's operation and his intention to kill Mussolini rather than taking him back alive to the Allies in Milan, these same theories then have to go on to describe the events that took place outside the Villa Belmonte at Giulino di Mezzegra in the afternoon as the mock execution of two corpses (sometimes even cited as body doubles).

The lack of any concrete proof of correspondence between Churchill and Mussolini other than the two letters actually written in May 1940 makes such conjectures appear even more threadbare.

Stripping away the many conspiracy theories, we are left with the likelihood that the killing of Mussolini and Petacci did take place in

Giulino di Mezzegra at around 4.10 p.m. on 28 April 1945 and that it was at the hands of Walter Audisio, Aldo Lampredi, and Michele Moretti, and possibly also of Luigi Canali, if Lada-Mocarski's second report is correct. The two foot soldiers, Guglielmo Cantoni and Giuseppe Frangi were witnesses, and the four members of the Insurrectional Committee - Luigi Longo, Sandro Pertini, Emilio Sereni, and Leo Valiani - the puppet masters.

In the prevailing atmosphere of 'Surrender or Die,' the threat that British and American secret agents might capture Mussolini and bring him to trial led them to decide to launch their own mission to kill him immediately.

Former partisan leader, Giovanni Pesce, wrote in his memoir, *Quando cessarono gli spari* (When the Shooting Stopped):

At least fifteen Anglo-American missions tried to free him from popular punishment to which he had been sentenced by the decision of the National Liberation Committee. [1]

The first Italian Prime Minister after the war, former partisan leader, Ferruccio Parri, made this revealing comment on the OSS mission of Captain Emilio Daddario:

There was a race between the executors of the National Liberation Committee's order, that is, 'Valerio' and 'Guido,' and the American agent who intended to reach Mussolini before he fell into our hands. A race that Daddario lost by a few hours, a difference of a few hours which decided the fate of Italy.

What then was the role of SOE? The British Ambassador, Sir Noel Charles, wrote to Winston Churchill on 13 June 1945:

The National Liberation Committee fully carried out their undertakings to the Allies in regard to the maintenance of law and order, the operation of public services, and the carrying out of measures for the protection of public and private property at the hands of the Germans.

He singled out four individuals for particular credit for the moderating influence they had exerted: Leo Valiani; Ferruccio Parri; Alfredo Pizzoni, the Committee's former President and head of the Finance Commission; and Max Salvadori:

Who for three months had participated actively in the work of the National Liberation Committee. As a former political prisoner of the Fascists he had the confidence of all parties and he did not hesitate to use his influence fully and courageously in preserving the unity of the Committee and in securing the carrying out of their undertakings. [2]

Salvadori revealed in his memoir, *The Labour and the Wounds*, that he had effectively told the members of the Liberation Committee that for several days they would have the widest discretion as regards their prisoners:

At one session of the CLNAI it was announced that the ex-dictator and other Fascist leaders had been arrested. Orders were given to bring the prisoners to Milan to be tried. To avoid misinterpretations, I made it clear once again that during the interim period the CLNAI was, in the eyes of the Allies, the government - that governmental powers, of course, included the administration of justice, but that as soon as the Allied troops arrived, the governing authority would automatically pass to the Allies, to whom all prisoners would have to be surrendered; as an Allied officer I was in a position to accept the surrender of regular troops or others recognised by the Allies; I could not do so in relation to civilians or to irregular formations…

The executions at Dongo were punishments for the greatest crime of all - that of robbing the Italian nation of its liberty. Because Italians had been deprived of their liberty, there had been aggressions in Africa, Spain, and the Balkans - the massacre of hundreds of thousands of people who had never done any harm to Italy or to Italians; there had been the steel pact with German Fascism and the consequent deaths of nearly half a million Italians in a war which the great majority of the Italians did not want, which had no justification, and which brought ruin and devastation to the entire peninsula. [3]

In 2004, a letter to the editor of *The Times* of London from former SOE agent, Thomas Smith, revealed the wartime dynamics:

An Italian television documentary is resurrecting once again the myths surrounding the killing of Mussolini in 1945.

I was a member of a Special Operations Executive (SOE) mission that was parachuted into Milan on 28 April 1945 to join the partisan group that was fighting the remaining Germans and Fascist militia that was still holding out in the city centre. In the first radio contact made with SOE HQ in Siena shortly after landing, we received and decoded a message that they believed that the partisan group we were with had captured Mussolini and that we should endeavour to secure and hold him until the main Allied Forces arrived.

Although the partisans then professed no knowledge of Mussolini's whereabouts, there is no doubt in my mind that, immediately they found out, a suitably armed party under a trusty lieutenant was dispatched to deal with the problem. It would have been done swiftly and ruthlessly. The partisans had no need of SOE executioners and their existence would be quite incompatible with the instructions we received. These were, of course, in line with the Allied policy on war criminals, arrest and trial. [4]

Leo Valiani, one of the four people who ordered the immediate killing of Mussolini, commented on those dramatic times on a number of occasions. In 1994, he told author Luciano Garibaldi:

I do not know whether all those killed at Dongo and at Giulino di Mezzegra had collaborated or not with the Germans. If yes, their execution was mandated by the National Liberation Committee decree. If the answer is no, then it was arbitrary. The sentence in any case should have been issued by a military court to be formed in accordance with the Committee decree. [5]

Valiani also told a news agency: 'The shooting of Claretta Petacci had never been ordered. We did not even know that she was with Mussolini at that time.'

In his wartime memoir, *Tutte le strade conducono a Roma* (All Roads Lead to Rome), published in 1995, Valiani related that the decision to execute Mussolini without trial was taken by the Insurrectional Committee on the night of 27-28 April and that it was made over the telephone owing to the urgency of the matter.

Just after Audisio's mission left for Dongo at dawn on 28 April, Valiani confirmed the order to shoot Mussolini to General Raffaele Cadorna and to the Christian Democrat Enrico Mattei, adjutant on the military committee and leader of the Catholic partisans.

Valiani argued later that the order was based on the delegated powers given to the Insurrectional Committee and on the provisions of Article Five on the Administration of Justice in the proclamation by the Liberation Committee at its final secret meeting on the morning of 25 April.

In 1996, he wrote a newspaper article headlined 'Leo Valiani Reveals the Dark Side of April '45.'

Claiming that the Communist Party hid the execution of the dictator, he wrote:

On the evening of 27 April, Sereni called me and asked if I agreed with executing Mussolini immediately. I gave my assent. After which I knew nothing more. I learned of the execution on the morning of 29 April when reading *l'Unità* and *l'Avanti*. I knew that the Communists always did things their own way, facing you with a fait accompli. I knew that they were treacherous allies. So I did not ask anything or question myself. [6]

In his memoir, Max Salvadori revealed his close links and friendship with Valiani. He wrote that he was successful in helping him and three or four other friends to leave Mexico for Italy in 1943 and that he met him again in the liberated south of the country later in the year.

Valiani then left to cross enemy lines to Rome and it was only when making his way to Milan in early 1945 that Salvadori learned that he was already in the north as an Action Party representative on the Liberation Committee.

Salvadori wrote that in April that year: 'Happily, light showed through the clouds now and again. I was glad when Valiani arrived since - as he knew who I really was - I could talk with him more freely than with others.' A revealing comment.

Valiani also provided most of the couriers to carry Salvadori's reports to SOE representatives in Switzerland.

Finally, Salvadori wrote that while the crucial meeting at the Archbishop's palace between Mussolini and his enemies on the Liberation Committee was being planned, 'Valiani was keeping me constantly informed on what was happening.'

The weekly report of SOE in Italy at the end of October 1944, conserved in the United Kingdom National Archives, spoke of Valiani as 'one of our helpers who has done a good job on the National Liberation Committee of Milan.' [7]

An internal SOE document from 30 May 1945 discussing the

possibility of maintaining a relationship with Valiani now that the war was over also pointed out: 'Any approach towards him must be very discreet, since in his current position within the Action Party he does not want his connection to British interests to be known.'

That relationship has been a matter of speculation and debate in Italy for many years, but documents in the National Archives prove conclusively that Valiani was secretly an agent of SOE from mid-1943 to 25 July 1945. His personnel file is reproduced here in full in Appendix C. [8]

It confirms that he was brought to the United Kingdom from Mexico in 1943 via the United States. His entry into the UK and subsequent stay was by special arrangement through SOE's London Headquarters and he was employed by its J Section owing to his motivation as an anti-fascist. Valiani left for North Africa disguised as a British soldier under their protection in August 1943 and subsequently became a prominent Resistance leader in Milan.

On 26 July 1945, Valiani signed a certificate marking the ending of his career as an SOE agent:

I, LEO VALIANI, hereby declare and certify that as from 25 July 1945 my association with No. 1 Special Force is officially terminated and that I have no claim, financial or otherwise, on No. 1 Special Force in Italy or elsewhere in respect of myself, my relatives or my friends.

Once the war was over, Valiani and fellow returnee Dino Gentili (alias 'Lieutenant Jessop') applied for permission to travel to Britain in their capacity of prominent Italian journalists. In support of their request, Lieutenant-Colonel Hedley Vincent, Officer Commanding No. 1 Special Force Field Liquidation Office, Milan, wrote on 2 August: 'These gentlemen are from the original group of anti-fascists who provided J Section London with so much trouble in early days. GAROSCI, TARCHIANI, LUSSU, etc., were the other members of the gang.' Aldo Garosci and Emilio Lussu were also SOE agents, with Emilio having as his partner and later wife the sister of Max Salvadori, Joyce (born Gioconda).

The Colonel's letter added: 'We should immediately wire London HQ to support their application and at same time to ensure that F.O. [Foreign Office], Home Office, and all concerned are acquainted with their past erratic activities under our auspices.'

The tone of the letter suggests some discord between SOE and these senior agents of Italian nationality. Leo Valiani in particular had ignored Allied orders involving the handing over of Mussolini in order for him to face trial and punishment and instead acted as one of the four members of the Insurrectional Committee who masterminded the order to kill him immediately.

An SOE agent since mid-1943, nevertheless Valiani followed his own agenda in the crucial last days of the war in Italy, as did many other leaders of the Resistance whose concerns completely diverged from those of the Allies.

The fate of the dictator and his leading supporters would therefore be determined by Italians and not by foreigners.

The outcome was inevitable: Between the 18th and the 28th of April 1945, Benito Mussolini made his last ever journey, from Gargnano to Giulino di Mezzegra, from life to death.

* * *

APPENDIX A

The Churchill-Mussolini Correspondence

Winston Churchill published the only letter that he actually wrote to Benito Mussolini, alongside the negative response, in his book, *Their Finest Hour*, pages 107-108, the second part of his monumental 1949 work, *The Second World War:*

16 May 1940

Prime Minister to *Signor* Mussolini

Now that I have taken up my office as Prime Minister and Minister of Defence I look back to our meetings in Rome and feel a desire to speak words of goodwill to you as Chief of the Italian nation across what seems to be a swiftly-widening gap. Is it too late to stop a river of blood from flowing between the British and Italian peoples? We can no doubt inflict grievous injuries upon one another and maul each other cruelly, and darken the Mediterranean with our strife. If you so decree, it must be so; but I declare that I have never been the enemy of Italian greatness, nor ever at heart the foe of the Italian lawgiver. It is idle to predict the outcome of the great battles now raging in Europe, but I am sure that whatever may happen on the Continent, England will go on to the end, even quite alone, as we have done before, and I believe with some assurance that we shall be aided in increasing measure by the United States, and, indeed, by all the Americas.

I beg you to believe that it is in no spirit of weakness or of fear that I make this solemn appeal, which will remain on record. Down the ages above all other calls comes the cry that the joint heirs of

Latin and Christian civilisation must not be ranged against one another in mortal strife. Hearken to it, I beseech you in all honour and respect, before the dread signal is given. It will never be given by us.

Two days later, Mussolini replied. Churchill wrote in his book: 'The response was hard. It had at least the merit of candour.'

18 May 1940

Signor Mussolini to Prime Minister

I reply to the message which you have sent me in order to tell you that you are certainly aware of grave reasons of an historical and contingent character which have ranged our two countries in opposite camps. Without going back very far in time I remind you of the initiative taken in 1935 by your Government to organise at Geneva sanctions against Italy, engaged in securing for herself a small space in the Africa sun without causing the slightest injury to your interests and territories or those of others. I remind you also of the real and actual state of servitude in which Italy finds herself in her own sea. If it was to honour your signature that your Government declared war on Germany, you will understand that the same sense of honour and of respect for engagements assumed in the Italian-German Treaty guides Italian policy today and tomorrow in the face of any event whatsoever.

In his book, Churchill concluded: 'From this moment we could have no doubt of Mussolini's intention to enter the war at his most favourable opportunity.'
   Italy declared war on Britain and France on 10 June 1940.

APPENDIX B

Churchill's Writings on Mussolini

In *Triumph and Tragedy,* the sixth and final part of the statesman's work, the only index reference to the dictator is 'Mussolini, Benito, death of, 460-1.' Churchill wrote that, after being captured:

On Communist instructions the *Duce* and his mistress were taken out in a car next day and shot. Their bodies, together with others, were sent to Milan and strung up head downwards on meat-hooks in a petrol station on the Piazzale Loreto, where a group of Italian partisans had lately been shot in public.

Such was the fate of the Italian dictator.

A photograph of the final scene was sent to me, and I was profoundly shocked.

Churchill blamed 'Communist instructions' for the executions rather than citing the three-party Insurrectional Committee. On 10 May 1945, he sent a telegram to Field Marshal Harold Alexander:

I have seen the photograph.

The man who murdered Mussolini made a confession, published in the *Daily Express*, gloating over the treacherous and cowardly method of his action. In particular, he said he shot Mussolini's mistress. Was she on the list of war criminals? Had he any authority from anybody to shoot this woman? It seems to me the cleansing hand of British military power should make inquiries on these points.

Churchill concluded his account with the words: 'But at least the world was spared an Italian Nuremberg.'

APPENDIX C

Special Operations Executive: Personnel Files (PF Series): Leo Weiczen, aka Leo Valiani, aka Giuseppe Federico - born 09.02.1909, The National Archives of the United Kingdom: HS 9/1569/4, 1939-1946

SECRET

HQ Ref No: CL/J/367
Date: 10 Aug '45

RECORD SHEET

1. Name: Valiani (This is his real name recently legalised)
2. Christian names: Leo
3. Aliases and Symbol: Leo: Giuseppe: Federico: Known openly until recently as Leo Weiczen
4. Date and place of birth: Fiume 9 Feb '09
5. Nationality: (a) Original: Italian (b) Present: Italian
6. If married: [Left blank]
7 Dependants: Is not legally married to the lady in Mexico to whom we have been paying monthly allowance. Eva Jay, c/o British Vice-Consul Mexico City.
8. Address: Via Benedetto Marcello 6, Milan
9. Group for which agent worked:
    (a) By whom was he engaged: J Section, London
    (b) Motive for undertaking work: Anti-fascist
    (c) Was he under written contract? No
10 Agent's remuneration: Check with London
11. Date of commencement of service: 1943
12. Date of termination of service: 25 July '45
13. Peacetime civilian employment: Journalist
14. Post-War employment:

(a) Does he propose to continue with his civilian employment? Yes.
(b) If not, what does he propose to do? Not applicable
(c) Is claimant's honesty and civilian occupation such that he could be employed after the war by BRITISH interest in trade or commerce, or similar capacity. If so, state nature of work suitable. (NOTE: - In obtaining this information care is to be taken not to inform, or imply, to the claimant that BRITISH interest are able or willing to use his services after the war.) Yes

15. Is it claimed that he has been prejudiced in his appointment or employable capacity by reason of his service with SOE? If so, give reason: No

16. What was the nature of the agent's employment? Give brief record of service with details of any special dangers incurred or any notable work performed.

The exact nature of the agent's duties in connection with the resistance are not known here, as he was infiltrated via Switzerland before the Armistice into the Milan area. He was engaged in resistance activity of a purely political nature and was closely connected with the CLNAI and as such contributed to its setting up and its work. He was responsible to V for reports on his resistance activity. Became one of the main Action Party leaders in Milan.

17. Any disability received by agent whilst so employed, with details of the circumstances in which disability occurred: Not applicable.

18. If deceased, give circumstances in which death occurred: Not applicable.

19. If is it claimed that the agent is likely to be victimised in any way (other than covered by para. 15) give the reason for such a claim and state by whom the victimisation is likely to be originated: Not applicable.

20. Degree of agent's responsibility (e.g. was he in command of a Mission, Group, etc?): Resistance leader in Milan.

21. General and any relevant information not allowed for above:

Subject was brought to UK from Mexico in '43 via USA. His entry into UK and subsequent stay there was by special arrangement through London HQ. As far as official British Govt. records show, he has never been to UK since he left disguised as British soldier for N. Africa in Aug '43 under our auspices. His present legal name of Valiani has never been used before by us in our dealings over him with military or civil authorities in UK. He does not desire repatriation to Mexico and has signed the Certificate attached at Appendix 'B.'

22. Recommendations:

(a) By BLO or Leader of Mission or Organisation: Left blank

(b) By Liquidation Office:

1. Facilitate his desired visit to UK for which he has already approached Press Attaché in Rome Embassy.

2. Ensure that London HQ have filed full details with competent offices of his existence whereby he will meet with no obstacles.

See attached letter Appendix 'A.'

Date: 2 Aug '45 … (Sgd.) H. Vincent Lt.-Col.

This page to be completed at H.Q.

Recommendations (Continued)

(c) By country section: As in Para. 22 (b)

Date: 14th August 1945 … Signed: R.T. Hewitt, Lt.-Col.

23. Give particulars of any recompense made on discharge, i.e. money payments, gifts in kind, certificate of service, honour, decoration, etc.

Letter to assist visit to U.K.: London asked to regularise position with competent U.K. offices.

24. Was the discharge on the standard form completed or not? No

No. 1 Special Force Field Liquidation Office, Milan

To: M I, HQ. SOM. ... Ref: PN/28 ... 2 August 1945

Subject (1) Leo Valiani
        (2) Dino Gentili

1. These gentlemen are from the original group of anti-fascists who provided J Section London with so much work in early days. GAROSCI, TARCHIANI, LUSSU, etc., were the other members of the gang.
2. Attached are record sheets for both.
3. Both have applied to Mike Stewart, Press Attaché, British Embassy, Rome, for visas to visit London in their capacity of prominent Italian journalists, which in fact they are.
4. We should immediately advise Press Attaché that both men were associated with us and that we support their application. They have already told P.A. that Special Force are vouching for them.
5. Rome Embassy will refer their application to London. We should immediately wire London HQ to support their application and at same time to ensure that F.O., Home Office and all concerned are acquainted with their past erratic activities under our auspices.
6. Dino Gentili is seeing P.A. early next week and it is hoped you

will do the necessary soonest poss.
7. Main points to remember are that:
(1) Leo Weiczen is now legally Leo Valiani.
(2) Dino Gentili spent many years in the UK in a regular way and then disappeared as Lieut. Jessop en route to Algiers.
8. Attached to record sheets are:
(1) Letter for forwarding to Leo's lady presumably referring to recent adjustments in her source of income.
(2) Signed certificate of liquidation of Leo.

(Sgd.) H. Vincent, Lt.-Col. ... O.C. No. 1 Special Force Field Liquidation Office Milan

To: H.Q., No. 1 Special Force, C.M.F. ... Appx. 'B'

I, LEO VALIANI, hereby declare and certify that as from 25 July 1945 my association with No. 1 Special Force is officially terminated and that I have no claim, financial or otherwise, on No. 1 Special Force in Italy or elsewhere in respect of myself, my relatives or my friends.

Milan ... Date: 26 July, 1945 ... (Sgd.) Leo Valiani.

ENDNOTES

Author's Note

1. The relevant British secret services in enemy territory were the Special Operations Executive (SOE), under its Italian cover name of No. 1 Special Force, and the Secret Intelligence Service (SIS, or MI6), run from the No. 1 Intelligence Unit in Bari. In *MI6, The History of the Secret Intelligence Service 1909-1949*, by Keith Jeffery, 'based on unprecedented, full and unrestricted access to the closed archives of the Service,' there are only five page references to Mussolini, none covering his execution.

Chapter 2 - Facing his Enemies

1. Some versions have people other than Marazza revealing the German contacts with the Resistance, depending upon who is telling the story.

Chapter 3 - Fascists in Flight

1. Another version of the story of the argument between Mussolini and Claretta Petacci states that it was she who stumbled on the carpet, hurting her knee.

Chapter 7 - The Capture of Mussolini

1. The main ranks of the Finance Guards in our story are either Brigadier (roughly equivalent to Sergeant or Sergeant Major in army terms) or Marshal (roughly equivalent to Warrant Officer). Official reports made by Finance Guards between May and August 1945 have informed this account. Set down after listening to the

narratives of local partisans (mostly given in dialect), the statements provide reliable testimony on the events of April 1945.

Chapter 9 - Moving Mussolini

1. Viganò, M. (1996). Arresto ed esecuzione di Mussolini nei rapporti della Guardia di finanza. *Italiano contemporanea*, no. 202, p. 131.

Chapter 12 - Partisan Plots in Milan

1. Bandini, *Le ultime 95 ore di Mussolini* (1968), p. 207.

Chapter 15 - The Execution

1. The bedroom occupied by Mussolini and Petacci at the De Maria house did have a window, but may have been shuttered during the brief visit of Audisio and his companions.
2. The autopsy on Mussolini was carried out on 30 April 1945 by Professor Mario Cattabeni and associates from the Institute of Forensic Medicine of the University of Milan. The report, number 7241, was headed: 'Benito Mussolini - shot at Giulino di Mezzegra on 28 April 1945. Execution by multiple shots.' Professor Cattabeni summarised his main conclusions in an article appearing in *Clinica Nuova*, 'Report of an Exceptional Autopsy,' 15 July - 1 August 1945.

He wrote that 'the only "vital" lesions were caused by gunshot wounds. In total, seven entry holes of bullets were identified, which were certainly produced during life.' Of these, four were clustered in the anterior-superior half of the left hemithorax, two in the upper and right sub-clavicular regions, and one in the suprahyoid region and right of the median line.

All the entry holes in the trunk corresponded posteriorly to exit holes. In addition, a pair of entry and exit holes was observed on the ulnar margin of the right forearm. In transthoracic procedures, the bullets pierced the left lung and caused the bursting rupture of the descending tract of the aorta.

Given these objective data, it is possible to establish:

1. That no injury was inflicted on Benito Mussolini before the execution.
2. That the execution took place with the executed man's chest facing the weapons.
3. That the death was immediate.
4. That in all likelihood there was a defensive act with the right arm during the execution.

Professor Cattabeni also noted that the injuries inflicted post-mortem were the most serious. In fact, there was a real traumatic collapse, partly due to gunshots and partly due to a contusive mechanism of extreme violence which is to be recognised in the precipitation that occurred due to the detachment of the suspended corpse. The Professor concluded: 'The physiognomic features were so deformed as to result in a real disfigurement that did not exist when the corpse was exposed on the square.'

No autopsy was carried out on Claretta Petacci on the orders of a certain Professor Pietro Bucalossi (Guido), who was acting on behalf of the Liberation Committee.

Chapter 17 - The American Investigation

1. Yale University Library: Reference: Libraries & Collections, Manuscripts & Archives, Manuscript 812.
2. Lada-Mocarski, V. (December 1945). The Last Three Days of Mussolini. *The Atlantic Monthly*, volume 176, number 6.

Chapter 18 - The Eyewitnesses

1. *Corriere Lombardo,* 25 February 1956.

Chapter 19 - Suspicious Deaths

1. *La Stampa,* 29 May 1957.

Chapter 20 - OSS Agents - 1

1. NARA, Record Group 226, *Report of the Events which Preceded and Led to the Capture of Mussolini,* 1 May 1945.

Chapter 21 - OSS Agents - 2

1. Mackenzie, *The Secret History of SOE, Special Operations Executive 1940-1945* (2002), p. 556.

Chapter 22 - OSS Agents - 3

1. Corvo, *The OSS in Italy 1942-1945, A Personal Memoir* (1990), p. 250. The Major served in Italy until November 1945.
2. *Ibid.,* p. 256.

Chapter 23 - SOE Agents - 1

1. Pickering, with Hart, *The Bandits of Cisterna* (1991), p. 2.
2. Salvadori, *The Labour and the Wounds* (2017), p. 312.

Chapter 24 - SOE Agents - 2

1. Salvadori, *op. cit.,* p. 314.

Chapter 25 - SOE Agents – 3

1. Lonati, *Quel 28 aprile, Mussolini e Claretta, la verità* (1994), pp. 49-50.
2. *Ibid.,* pp. 51-53.
3. *Ibid.,* pp. 55-56.
4. The article in *The Times* by Rome Correspondent Richard Owen on 28 August 2004, entitled 'Mussolini killed "on Churchill's orders by British agents," included an interview with SOE specialist Christopher Woods, who said that Lonati's story was a total fabrication, adding: 'It's just love of conspiracy making. The leaders of the Resistance in Milan, particularly the left-wing parties, decided that Mussolini should be killed before the Allies arrived.'

The article in *The Independent* by Peter Popham on 29 August 2004, entitled 'Churchill "ordered killing of Mussolini," included a comment by Mussolini biographer Nicholas Farrell on the 'Churchill-Mussolini correspondence': 'All the letters that have emerged are crude forgeries. The only genuine letters that exist between Churchill and Mussolini are two, written just before the war in which Churchill begs Mussolini not to go into the war.'

5. Lonati, *op. cit.,* p. 21.
6. *Ibid.,* p. 23.

Chapter 26 - Allied Orders

1. The term 'United Nations' in the agreement refers to the alliance of wartime Allies, and not to the present day inter-governmental organisation of the same name, which aims to maintain international peace and security (founded in 1945).

Chapter 27 - General Cadorna's Orders

1. Cadorna, *La Riscossa* (1976), pp. 315-316.

Chapter 28 - Partisan Orders

1. *La Stampa*, 23 May 1957.
2. Pesce, *Quando cessarono gli spari* (2009), pp. 129-130.
3. *Ibid.,* p. 132.

29 - Who Ordered the Killings?

1. Salvadori, *op. cit.,* p. 195.

30 - The Italian Solution

1. Pesce, *op. cit.,* p. 123.
2. TNA: FO 371/49771, *Political Situation in Italy*, 1945.
3. Salvadori, *op. cit.,* pp. 315-316.
4. Thomas Smith, 'Mussolini's End,' Letter to *The Times*, 4 September 2004. TNA HS9/1384/2: Thomas Joseph Smith - born 22.04.1923, 1939-1946, reveals that he was a sergeant who served in Palestine, Yugoslavia, and finally Milan.
5. Garibaldi (2004), *Mussolini, The Secrets of his Death*, p. 86.
6. Valiani, L. (1996). Leo Valiani racconta i lati oscuri dell' aprile '45. Il Pci nascose l' esecuzione del duce, *Corriere della Sera,* 10 July 1996.
7. 'Progress report week ending 29 October 1944,' in TNA WO 208/4554, Intelligence situation reports and reports on partisan movements, 1 June 1944 - 30 June 1945.
8. TNA: HS 9/1516/1, Leo Valiani, aka Leo Weiczen - born 09.02.1909.

LEADING PERSONALITIES

Walter Audisio (Colonel Valerio) Accountant, politician, wartime partisan officer attached to the Military Committee of the Resistance. Self-avowed killer of Mussolini and Petacci

Francesco Maria Barracu Italian Army Colonel, holder of the Gold Medal for Military Valour, wartime Under-Secretary to the Presidency of the Council of the Italian Social Republic (RSI). Shot in Dongo on 28 April 1945

Pier Luigi Bellini delle Stelle (Pedro) Florentine nobleman, lawyer, wartime partisan commandant of the 52nd Garibaldi Brigade Luigi Clerici on Lake Como

Virginio Bertinelli Socialist lawyer, politician, Prefect of Como on the Liberation

Fritz Birzer Businessman, wartime Waffen SS Second-Lieutenant with the anti-aircraft unit *3-II Flak Einheit* of the Panzer Grenadier Division SS *Reichsführer*, commandant of Mussolini's German escort during his last 10 days

Guido Buffarini-Guidi Veteran Fascist, former Minister of the Interior, captured by the partisans on 26 April 1945 and shot in Milan on 10 July

Giorgio Buffelli Brigadier of the Finance Guards of Dongo, participant in the capture and imprisonment of Mussolini

Raffaele Cadorna Italian Army General, politician, wartime head of the Military Committee of the Resistance from 1944 to 1945

Luigi Canali (Captain Neri) Accountant, engineer officer in the Italian Army, wartime Chief of Staff of the 52nd Garibaldi Brigade Luigi Clerici. Killed in mysterious circumstances on the night of 7-8 May 1945

Guglielmo Cantoni (Sandrino) Member of the 52nd Garibaldi Brigade Luigi Clerici, one of the guards of Mussolini and Petacci at Bonzanigo

Winston S. Churchill Soldier, journalist, politician, wartime Prime Minister from 1940 to 1945 (and from 1951 to 1955 in peacetime)

Max Corvo Journalist, publisher, wartime Operations Officer of the Italian Secret Intelligence Branch of the Office of Strategic Services, 1943-1945

Elena Cucciati Curti Daughter of Benito Mussolini and Angela Cucciati Curti

Emilio Daddario Lawyer, politician, wartime Assistant Operations Officer of the Italian Secret Intelligence Branch of the Office of Strategic Services, 1943-1945. Head of a mission to capture Mussolini and liaise with the National Liberation Committee in Milan

Cosimo Maria De Angelis Italian Army Major, wartime leader of the Como Military Committee of the Resistance

Giacomo and Lia De Maria The couple from Bonzanigo in whose house Mussolini and Petacci spent their last night

Giovanni Dessy Italian Royal Navy Captain, wartime OSS agent sent to obtain the surrender of Mussolini, his leading supporters, and all Fascist forces arriving in Como

Allen Welsh Dulles Lawyer, diplomat, wartime Director of OSS Switzerland from 1942 to 1945 and future head of the Central Intelligence Agency

Hans Fallmeyer German Lieutenant of the *Luftwaffe's* radar unit, the *Luftnachrichten-Regiment 200*, de facto commandant of the convoy composed of Germans in retreat and Fascists in flight

Giuseppe Frangi (Lino) Member of the 52nd Garibaldi Brigade Luigi Clerici, one of the guards of Mussolini and Petacci at Bonzanigo. Killed in mysterious circumstances on the night of 4-5 May 1945

Dante Gorreri (Guglielmo) Plumber, union activist, politician, wartime Secretary of the underground Communist Party of Como from 1944 to 1945

Rodolfo Graziani Marshal of Italy, former military governor of Somalia, wartime Minister of National Defence of the Italian Social Republic and commandant of Army Group Liguria. Captured by the OSS and saved from certain death at the hands of the partisans

Salvatore Guastoni Italian Army Captain, lawyer, stockbroker, wartime OSS agent sent with Giovanni Dessy to obtain the surrender of Mussolini, his leading supporters, and all Fascist forces arriving in Como

Aldo Icardi Lawyer, wartime American Army Lieutenant and OSS agent active in Lombardy

Donald Pryce Jones (Scotti) American journalist, wartime head of OSS Lugano under the cover of Vice-Consul, influential link with the partisans

Otto Kisnat German agent of the *Sicherheitsdienst (SD)*, the secret security service, who led his squad in Mussolini's convoy

Valerian Lada-Mocarski White Russian, naturalised American, lawyer, banker, wartime senior OSS agent responsible for reporting on 'The Last Days of Mussolini and his Ministers'

Aldo Lampredi (Guido Conti) Cabinet maker, politician, wartime collaborator of the Communist leader in the north, Luigi Longo, sent with Walter Audiso to lead the partisan mission to Dongo in order to kill Mussolini

Orfeo Landini (Piero) Industrial technician, Italian Army Second-Lieutenant, wartime second in command of the partisan platoon accompanying Audisio and Lampredi to Dongo

Urbano Lazzaro (Bill) Officer of the Finance Guards of Chiavenna, joined the 52nd Garibaldi Brigade Luigi Clerici and on 27 April 1945 personally captured Mussolini in Dongo

Bruno Giovanni Lonati (Giacomo) Italian engineer, writer, wartime commandant of the 110th, 111th, and 112th Garibaldi Brigades in Milan. Self-avowed killer of Mussolini

Luigi Longo (Gallo, Italo) Veteran of the Spanish Civil War, politician, wartime Italian Communist leader in the north, Vice-Commandant of the Military Committee and member of the National Liberation Committee

Alfredo Mordini (Riccardo) Railwayman, veteran of the Spanish Civil War, wartime partisan officer of the 3rd Aliotta Division, leader of the platoon sent to Dongo

Michele Moretti (Pietro Gatti) Footballer, union activist, wartime partisan Political Commissar of the 52nd Garibaldi Brigade Luigi Clerici, provider of local knowledge to the squad from Milan

Anna Maria Mussolini Youngest daughter of Benito and Rachele Mussolini, radio personality

Benito Mussolini Soldier, journalist, politician, creator of Italian Fascism. Leader of the Italian Social Republic from September 1943 to April 1945 (and Prime Minister of the Kingdom of Italy from October 1922 to July 1943). Shot in Mezzegra on 28 April 1945

Rachele Mussolini Second Wife of Benito Mussolini

Romano Mussolini Youngest son of Benito and Rachele Mussolini, pianist, painter, film producer. Author of *Il Duce, Il mio padre* (The *Duce*, My Father)

Vittorio Mussolini Eldest son of Benito and Rachele Mussolini, film critic and producer

Ferruccio Parri (Maurizio) Leading member of the Action Party, wartime Vice-Commandant of the Military Committee and member of the National Liberation Committee. Italian Prime Minister from June to December 1945

Alessandro Pavolini Journalist, veteran Fascist, founder of the Black Brigades. Shot in Dongo on 28 April 1945

Alessandro (known as Sandro) Pertini Lawyer, politician, wartime Socialist member of the National Liberation Committee, holder of the Gold Medal for Military Valour. President of the Italian Republic from 1978 to 1985

Giovanni Pesce (Visone) Miner, veteran of the Spanish Civil War, wartime leader of partisan action groups in the Milan area

Clara (known as Claretta) Petacci Lover of Benito Mussolini. Shot in Mezzegra on 28 April 1945

Marcello Petacci Doctor brother of Claretta Petacci. Shot in Dongo on 28 April 1945

Massimo (Max William) Salvadori-Paleotti (Speranza) Anglo-Italian historian, writer, wartime British Army Lieutenant-Colonel and Special Operations Executive Liaison Officer to the National Liberation Committee of the Resistance from March to May 1945

Giovanni Sardagna Baron of Hohenstein, wartime aide-de-camp to General Cadorna and his representative in Como during the final days of the war

Antonio Scappin (Carlo) Brigadier of the Finance Guards of Gera Lario, participant in the capture and imprisonment of Mussolini

Ildefonso Schuster Cardinal Archbishop of Milan from 1929 to 1954, mediator at the meeting between Mussolini and the Resistance leaders on 25 April 1945

Emilio Sereni Historian of Italian agriculture, writer, politician, wartime Communist member of the National Liberation Committee

Oscar Sforni Textile worker, wartime Secretary of the provincial National Liberation Committee of Como

Angelo Tarchi Industrialist, wartime Minister of Industrial Production and Corporate Economy, captured by the partisans on 26 April 1945 and eventually amnestied by the Italian State

Palmiro Togliatti Journalist, politician, Communist leader.

Peter Tompkins Famous American journalist and author, wartime OSS agent in North Africa, Italy, and Germany

Giuseppina Tuissi (Gianna) Courier of the 52nd Garibaldi Brigade Luigi Clerici, lover of Luigi Canali (Captain Neri). Killed by her companions on 23 June 1945

Leo Valiani (previously Leo Weiczen) Journalist, politician, brought to Italy from Mexico by SOE in 1943, Action Party member of the National Liberation Committee

Pietro Vergani (Fabio) Worker, union activist, politician, wartime partisan Regional Commandant in Lombardy and Vice-Commandant of the Military Committee of the Resistance

Karl Wolff SS-*Obergruppenführer* and General of the Military SS, Highest SS and Police Leader, Military Plenipotentiary of the German Armed Forces in Italy, Commander of the Rear Military Area and the Military Administration, and Himmler's personal representative. Leader of German generals in Italy secretly negotiating a peace agreement with the Allies

- The battle names adopted by partisans are shown in brackets -

BIBLIOGRAPHY

Audisio, W., *In nome del popolo italiano* (Milan: Teti editore, 1975)
Bandini, F., *Le ultime 95 ore di Mussolini* (Milan: Mondadori, 1968)
Battaglia, R., *The Story of the Italian Resistance* (London: Odhams Press, 1957)
Bellini delle Stelle, P. L., Lazzaro, U., *Dongo, ultima azione* (Milan: Mondadori, 1962)
Berrettini, M., *La Resistenza italiana e lo Special Operations Executive brittanico (1943-1945)* (Florence: Casa Editrice Le Lettere, 2014)
Bollone, P. B., *Le ultime ore di Mussolini* (Milan: Mondadori, 2006)
Cadorna, R., *La Riscossa* (Milan: Bietti, 1976)
Cavalleri, G., Giannantoni, F., Cereghino, M. J., *Gli ultimi giorni di Benito Mussolini nei documenti dei servizi segreti americani (1945-1946)* (Milan: Garzanti, 2009)
Churchill, W. S., *The Second World War, Volume II, Their Finest Hour* (Harmondsworth: Penguin Books, 1985); *Volume VI, Triumph and Tragedy* (Harmondsworth: Penguin Books, 1985)
Collotti, E., Sandri, R., and Sessi, F., *Dizionario della Resistenza* (Turin: Einaudi, 2006)
Corvo, M., *The OSS in Italy 1942-1945, A Personal Memoir* (New York: Praeger, 1990)
Dulles, A. W., *The Secret Surrender* (Guilford, United States: The Lyons Press, 2006)
Fucci, F., *Spie per la libertà, I Servizi segreti della Resistenza italiana* (Milan: Mursia, 1983)
Garibaldi, L., *Mussolini, The Secrets of his Death* (New York: Enigma Books, 2004)
Icardi, A., *American Master Spy* (Pittsburgh: Stalwart Enterprises, 1954)
Jeffery, K., *MI6, The History of the Secret Intelligence Service*

1909-1949 (London: Bloomsbury, 2011)

Lonati, B. G., *Quel 28 aprile, Mussolini e Claretta: la verità* (Milan: Mursia, 1994)

Mackenzie, W., *The Secret History of SOE, The Special Operations Executive 1940-1945* (London: St Ermin's Press, 2002)

Milza, P., *Gli ultimi giorni di Mussolini* (Milan: Longanesi, 2011)

Mussolini, R., *Il Duce mio padre* (Milan: BUR Storia, 2004)

Pesce, G., *Quando cessarono gli spari, 23 aprile-6 maggio 1945: la liberazione di Milano* (Milan: Feltrinelli, 2009)

Pickering, W., with Hart, A., *The Bandits of Cisterna* (London: Leo Cooper, 1991)

Piffer, T., *Gli Alleati e la Resistenza italiana* (Bologna: Il Mulino, 2010)

Pisanò, G., *Gli ultimi cinque secondi di Mussolini, Un' inchiesta giornalistica durata quarant' anni* (Milan: Il Saggiatore, 2009)

Salvadori, M., *The Labour and the Wounds: A Personal Chronicle of One Man's Fight for Freedom* (Atascadero: Trovatello Press, 2017)

Stafford, D., *Mission Accomplished, SOE and Italy 1943-45* (London: Lume Books, 2020)

Tompkins, P., *Dalle carte segreti del Duce* (Milan: Il Saggiatore, 2010); *L'altra Resistenza* (Milan: Il Saggiatore, 2009)

Tudor, M., *Among the Italian Partisans:* (Stroud: Fonthill Media, 2016); *At War in Italy 1943-1945: True Adventures in Enemy Territory* (Newtown: Emilia Publishing, 2007)

Valiani, L., *Tutte le strade conducono a Roma* (Bologna: Il Mulino, 1995)

Various Authors, *Gli americani e la guerra di liberazione in Italia, Office of Strategic Services (OSS) e la Resistenza italiana* (Rome: Presidenza del Consiglio dei Ministri, 1995); *No. 1 Special Force and Italian Resistance* (Bologna: University of Bologna, 1990)

Whittle, P., *One Afternoon at Mezzegra, Mussolini's Last Journey*

(London: W. H. Allen, 1969)

Newspaper Articles

Corriere della Sera. (10 July 1996). Valiani, L. Leo Valiani racconta i lati oscuri dell' aprile '45
Corriere Lombardo (25 February 1956) on Moretti
La Repubblica (20 July 2010). Uno 007 in Sicilia, on Daddario
La Stampa (23 May 1957). Cadorna's evidence; (29 May 1957). On Audisio's expenses
L'Unità (23 January 1996) on Lampredi's report
The Independent (29 August 2004). Popham, P. Churchill 'ordered killing of Mussolini'
The Times (28 August 2004). Owen, R. Mussolini killed 'on Churchill's orders by British agents;' (4 September 2004) Smith, T. Mussolini's End, letter to the editor
L'Arena' di Verona (1 and 3 March, 1981). Pierre-Jouvet. J. Fritz Birzer: Ecco la verità sugli ultimi giorni di Mussolini

Magazine Articles

Bollettino d'Archivio (February 2007). Guardia di Finanza Museo Storico, Roma. La cattura di Mussolini. Anno 1, no. 1, pp. 79-135
Clinica Nuova (15 July - 1 August 1945). Cattabeni, C. M. Rendiconto di una necroscopia d'eccezione
Italiano contemporanea (March 1996). Viganò, M. Arresto ed esecuzione di Mussolini nei rapporti della Guardia di finanza. No. 202, pp. 113-138
The Atlantic Monthly (December 1945). Lada-Mocarski, V. The Last Three Days of Mussolini. Volume 176, no. 6.

If you've enjoyed reading this book, a review on Amazon or Goodreads would be much appreciated.